Jim,

Enjoy dining in Georgia —

Sharon & Alan

Dining in
HISTORIC
GEORGIA

A Restaurant Guide With Recipes

by Marty Godbey

Illustrations by James Asher

McClanahan
Publishing House

Library of Congress Catalog Card Number: 92 064253
International Standard Book Number: 0-913383-25-2
Cover photograph: Billie's Blue Willow Inn, Social Circle, Georgia

Illustrations by James Asher
Back cover photograph by Frank Godbey
Cover design, cover photograph and book layout by James Asher Graphics

Manufactured in the United States of America

All book order correspondence should be addressed to:
McClanahan Publishing House, Inc.
P. O. Box 100
Kuttawa, Kentucky 42055
(502)388-9388
1-800-544-6959

INTRODUCTION

From its very beginning in the mind of James Edward Oglethorpe, the idea, the colony, and the State of Georgia have grasped the imagination. Whether the mental picture is one of ancient live oaks wreathed with moss, sprawling acres of cotton and peaches, slender pines reaching for the sky, or icy streams rushing through mountain passes, Georgia's variety is unforgettable.

Just as diverse are the people who settled Georgia: the colonists in 1732, not the debtors of persistent myth, but carefully chosen "worthy poor"; German Salzbergers and Moravians and English Jews seeking religious freedom; Scottish Highlanders escaping political intolerance; Virginians and Carolinians hoping for richer land; Africans brought in bondage; and, too often overlooked, Native Americans, Creeks and Cherokee, who were gradually, then forcibly dispossessed of lands they had settled before Europeans came.

Georgians have had to overcome hardships of yellow fever, isolation, injustice, over-farmed land, tragic war, and the humiliation of living in an occupied country. Resistance to change slowed economic growth until recently, but perhaps that very stubbornness forged the Georgian character.

We are individuals, and we know how to live!

In an often unfriendly climate, we have made ourselves comfortable with porches and high ceilings; we have utilized long growing seasons to surround ourselves with verdant beauty and homegrown bounty; and we have learned to make any gathering an occasion.

To many, the word "Georgia" is always followed by "hospitality." We have always shared what we had, even under conditions of poverty; in times of plenty, our tables are laden, and visitors are pressed to indulge themselves.

And the food we eat and offer to others is arguably the best in the world. Georgia products—corn, pork, greens, poultry, legumes, peanuts and pecans, sweet potatoes, game and seafood—can be prepared in endless ways. Combining traditional ingredients, learned techniques, and foods relatively new to the area can result in sparkling new tastes, but it is still possible to feast on foods our grandparents knew and loved.

Some of Georgia's most exciting food may be found in equally interesting places, many closely connected with events and people that shaped the state. Homes of statesmen, farmers, craftsmen, and industrialists have been restored or refurbished and converted into restaurants. Resorts where city-dwellers "took the waters" or avoided summer heat continue to provide stress-free relaxation.

Banks, drugstores, and mercantile establishments have been adapted as restaurants, preserving their unique qualities and offering patrons a little history with their food.

Such unlikely structures as train stations, a casino, a church, a factory, and a "millionaire's club" now offer food to the public, and elegant old hotels have been revitalized, giving visitors an opportunity to observe at first hand some of the places their ancestors took for granted.

There are no two alike, and because they belong to people who value the past enough to utilize old buildings, with the attendant inconveniences, they are all very special.

A visit to any of Georgia's restaurants in historic buildings is well repaid, for an appreciation of the past is as easily absorbed as the excellent food, and the diner leaves satisfied in more ways than one.

Using *Dining In Historic Georgia* as a travel guide

Dining in Historic Georgia began in file folders, as notes about restaurants in historic buildings were accumulated over a period of years. Gathered from advertisements, history books, old automobile guides, word-of-mouth reports, and personal experience, these notes grew into computer files.

Dining in Historic Georgia is a continuation of a series of travel guides to restaurants in historic buildings that includes *Dining in Historic Kentucky, Dining in Historic Ohio, Dining In Historic Tennessee,* and *Dining In The Historic South.* The same criteria were used in this book as in its predecessors: restaurants were chosen on a basis of historic, architectural, and culinary interest (frequently all three) coupled with business stability.

Georgia's tradition of hospitality, carried out in her restaurants, made selection difficult; ultimately, choices were made on preservation/restoration grounds. Of the 48 buildings which house the restaurants included, 25 are on the National Register of Historic Places; three more are part of National Historic Landmarks. In addition, those chosen all met the final requirement: they are places a first-time visitor would describe enthusiastically to friends.

The author, often with companions, ate anonymously in every restaurant at least once, ensuring the same treatment any hungry traveler might receive. No restaurant paid to be included or was told of the project until asked to participate. Restaurant owners and managers have been enthusiastic, gracious, and cooperative, some providing recipes that had never before been disclosed.

As an aid to travelers, restaurants are grouped (roughly northeast, northwest, etc.,) then listed north to south. Resource information between text and recipes provides addresses and telephone numbers, and all travelers are encouraged to call before driving long distances.

Laws governing the sale of alcoholic beverages vary greatly. If beverages are available, it will be so indicated in the resource information; many dry areas permit "brown-bagging" or bringing your own, but it would be wise to inquire ahead.

Symbols used for brevity include charge card references: AE=American Express, CB=Carte Blanche, DC=Diner's Club,

DS=Discover, JCB=Japan Credit Bureau, MC=Master Card, V=Visa.

Most of these restaurants would fall into the "moderate" category of expensiveness; an effort was made to include all price ranges. Using dinner entrée prices as a gauge, dollar signs ($) are used to indicate reasonable ($), moderate ($$), and more expensive ($$$). Luncheon prices are usually significantly lower, and the amount spent in any restaurant is increased by the "extras" ordered, i.e., appetizers, drinks, and side orders.

In traditional Southern service, main dishes are frequently accompanied by vegetable(s), salad, and often dessert, and in these cases, the price is counted as an entrée price.

Few of these restaurants would be considered expensive by East or West Coast standards; if cost is a determining factor, however, most restaurants will gladly provide a price range over the telephone.

Visitors are cautioned that some of the restaurants in *Dining in Historic Georgia* have a large local following, and their busy seasons may be determined by local events not familiar to non-residents. To avoid disappointment, CALL AHEAD FOR RESERVATIONS.

A WORD OF CAUTION: when *Dining in Historic Georgia* went to press, the 404 telephone area code previously in use in North and West Georgia had just been changed to 706 except for Atlanta and its environs. Some areas, however, contested the change, and final determination had not been made in a few cases. If you have difficulty in reaching a restaurant in the Greater Atlanta periphery, try the other area code or ask for assistance.

TABLE OF CONTENTS

Dining In
HISTORIC
GEORGIA

SAUTEE• •TURNERVILLE
•CLARKESVILLE
TOCCOA•
•ADAIRSVILLE   LAVONIA•
•ROME   GAINESVILLE•
MARIETTA•   •ROSWELL
VININGS•   •ATHENS
ATLANTA• •STONE MTN.
DECATUR• •SOCIAL CIRCLE   •WASHINGTON
COVINGTON• •RUTLEDGE
CARROLLTON•   AUGUSTA•
•NEWNAN
•GRIFFIN
•LaGRANGE
•WARM SPRINGS
•MACON
•COLUMBUS •PERRY   STATESBORO•
•HAWKINSVILLE
•AMERICUS   SAVANNAH•
•RADIUM SPRINGS •DOUGLAS
•JEKYLL
ISLAND
•VALDOSTA   •ST. MARYS

RESTAURANTS

THE STOVALL HOUSE
Sautee

People have always appreciated the lovely Sautee (pronounced saw-tee) and Nacoochee (nah-COO-chee) valleys, near the headwaters of the Chattahoochee River. Relics show ice-age occupancy; later, in the Nacoochee Valley, the Cherokee town of Little Chota was located at the intersection of two important Indian trails.

The Cherokee sided with the British during the American Revolution, and in retaliation for an uprising, Continentals destroyed Little Chota in 1776.

After Georgia acquired the land in the Indian Cession of 1819, settlers moved in; gold was discovered in 1828, and the Cherokee were driven from their homes.

When gold and lumber played out, residents' lives centered around agriculture. More than two dozen nineteenth- and early twentieth-century structures remain in the valleys; the Nacoochee Valley was placed on the National Register of Historic Places in 1980; the Sautee Valley in 1986.

One of the oldest houses, probably built by Moses Harshaw about 1837, was enlarged by its second owner, Lucius Lamar. Purchased in 1895 by W.I. Stovall, it acquired a sleeping porch and rear extension during his occupancy. A story-and-a-half frame house with wide verandas and high ceilings, it was placed on the National Register in 1984.

Now a country inn owned by "Ham" and Carolyn Schwartz, Stovall House has received numerous awards for their painstaking restoration. Panoramic views from the veranda and crackling fires beneath walnut mantels provide serenity, but the food is exciting.

Stressing freshness—some vegetables from local gardens—and variety, everything is prepared from "the ground up." Enhanced by homemade breads and muffins, meals provide exciting contrasts—chilled Misty Melon Soup, savory cheese/herb stuffed chicken, zesty devilled carrots, and matchless Chocolate Raspberry Mousse with black raspberry liqueur.

Whether you stay for a meal, overnight, or a week, your body and your soul will be enriched by a visit to what has been described as "the most beautiful spot in the world."

The Stovall House is 5 miles east of Helen and 17 miles west of Clarkesville, off GA 17 about 2 miles on GA 255N. Dinner is served from 5:30 to 8:30 p.m.; April through November, Tuesday through

Sunday; December through March, Thursday through Sunday. Sunday brunch is served year round, 10 a.m. to 2 p.m. (706)878-3355. Dress is casual, reservations are recommended, and October is EXTREMELY busy. There are 5 overnight units. MC,V, Personal checks. ($$)

PORK AND CHINESE VEGETABLE PHYLLO

1 pound pork roast, diced
Oil
⅛ cup soy sauce
⅛ cup sherry
½ teaspoon granulated garlic
½ cup diagonally sliced
  carrots

1½ cups diagonally sliced
  celery
½ small white cabbage,
  finely sliced
1 medium onion, finely sliced
Phyllo pastry sheets
Melted butter
Sauce*

In skillet, sauté meat in oil until lightly browned; add seasonings and vegetables and cook, covered, about 5 minutes. For each roll, use 2 sheets phyllo, brushing each with butter, then stacking. Center ½ cup filling on sheet, about 1" from bottom edge. Fold over sides, then roll away from you. Repeat with remaining filling. Place rolls on greased pan, loose end down, brush tops with butter, and bake at 350 degrees 10 to 15 minutes, until slightly brown. Serve with warm sauce*.

*Sauce: in saucepan, mix ½ teaspoon butter, 1 Tablespoon corn starch, 1 cup water, ¼ cup cider vinegar, ½ cup brown sugar, and ½ teaspoon ginger. Simmer 15 minutes.

VEGETABLE CASSEROLE

½ cup chopped onion
1 pound zucchini,
  yellow squash, or broccoli,
  thinly sliced
Butter

3 eggs
1 pound ricotta cheese
2 cups grated sharp cheddar
3 Tablespoons flour
Dash nutmeg
Grated Parmesan for topping

In skillet, sauté vegetables in butter. Mix remaining ingredients, then combine with vegetables in baking dish. Sprinkle with Parmesan and bake at 375 degrees 35 to 40 minutes.

APPLE-NUT MUFFINS

4 cups flour
4 teaspoons baking powder
2 teaspoons salt
¼ cup melted butter

2 eggs
½ teaspoon vanilla
2 cups milk
1¼ cups diced apples
½ cup chopped walnuts

In bowl, mix dry ingredients. Mix liquids, pour into drys and stir until moistened. Add apples and walnuts, stirring just enough to combine. Spoon into well-greased muffin tins and bake at 375 degrees 20 to 25 minutes. Yields 20 to 24 muffins.

APPLE-PRALINE PIE

Unbaked deep-dish pie shell
1½ cups sugar
¼ cup flour
½ teaspoon nutmeg
½ teaspoon cinnamon

2 eggs, beaten
½ cup melted margarine
1 teaspoon vanilla
3 cups peeled,
    chopped apples
½ cup chopped pecans

In bowl, mix sugar with flour and spices. Add wet ingredients, stir in apples, and pour into pie shell. Bake at 425 degrees 15 minutes. Sprinkle pecans on top and press into pie; bake at 350 degrees 25 minutes, or until set.

GLEN-ELLA SPRINGS INN
Turnerville, near Clarkesville

Habersham County was named for colorful patriot Joseph Habersham, of Savannah, an organizer of Georgia's first Revolutionary council. A Colonel in the Continental Army and a member of the Georgia Convention that ratified the Constitution, he served as Postmaster General under our first three Presidents.

Savannah's summer heat and fevers were of serious concern to early residents, and Joseph Habersham was one of the first to summer in the cool North Georgia mountains. He built a house near Clarkesville, and by the 1830s, the area was a popular resort.

Adjacent to Glen and Ella Davidson's 1875 farmhouse, on what was then the main road, a house built in 1890 accommodated paying guests. In 1905, the two were connected, creating a sprawling frame hotel with two-story porches on both sides. Ella's good food and a "healing" spring assured the success of the hotel, which remained in operation until the 1920s, and in the family until the 1950s.

It had deteriorated when Bobby and Barrie Aycock bought it in 1986, but Bobby, a contractor, restored heart pine interiors and found fieldstone fireplaces hidden beneath stucco; only the porches needed to be replaced, and electricity and plumbing were installed for the first time. The Glen-Ella Springs Inn opened in 1987, and was placed on the National Register in 1990.

Cozy fires, comfortable furnishings, and the restful atmosphere again attract guests to the cool mountains, where flavors from Barrie's herb garden enhance the Inn's "sophisticated American-Continental" cuisine. Fresh mountain trout, local fruits and vegetables, and delicious homemade breads and desserts are featured—you can get a picnic from the Inn's Cottage Garden Shop to carry on a hike, then dine at the Inn.

At dinner, begin with gazpacho, or fresh vegetable fritters, then, after Tomato-Basil Fettuccine with Roasted Eggplant, Trout Pecan, Cajun Pasta (spicy, with shrimp) or popular rack of lamb, consider Apple Bread Pudding with cinnamon ice cream and butterscotch sauce, or Chocolate Peanut Butter Cookie Torte: wedges of a huge cookie, topped with vanilla ice cream and ladled with chocolate.

Glen-Ella Springs Inn and Conference Center is 2½ miles off US 441 on Bear Gap Road at Turnerville, between Clarkesville and Clayton. June 1 to mid-November it is open Tuesday through Sunday for dinner, 6 to

9 p.m., and for Sunday brunch buffet 11:30 a.m. to 2 p.m. Lunch is served only on Easter and Mothers' Day. Winter hours vary; call for reservations. (404)754-7295; (800)552-3479. Dress is casual, reservations are strongly suggested (a MUST for weekend dinner), and busiest time is "leaf season" in autumn. There are 16 overnight units. AE,MC,V. ($$)

HERB GRILLED CHICKEN*

Herb butter* - prepare ahead
Basting butter** -
  prepare ahead

Four 8-ounce chicken
  breast halves, skinned

Grill chicken over medium coals 8 to 10 minutes each side, basting often with basting butter.** Remove to plate and top each breast with 1 teaspoon herb butter.* Serves 4.

*Herb butter: combine in food processor ½ cup softened butter, 2 Tablespoons mixed fresh herbs (basil, thyme, dill, oregano, etc.), 1 Tablespoon grated Parmesan cheese, ¼ teaspoon minced garlic, ⅛ teaspoon salt, ⅛ teaspoon pepper. Chill or freeze.

**Basting butter: mix ⅓ cup melted butter or margarine with ¼ cup mixed herbs (as above).

TROUT PECAN*

1½ to 2 pounds trout filets,
  skin on
Coating mix*
Margarine

2 limes, halved
Minced mixed fresh herbs
  (see above)
¼ cup toasted chopped pecans

Dredge trout in coating mix. In large non-stick skillet, heat ⅛" margarine; add trout skin side up and sauté over medium-high heat until golden brown on flesh side. Place filets skin down in shallow oven-proof pan. Over each fish, squeeze ½ lime, and sprinkle with

1 Tablespoon herbs and 1 Tablespoon pecans. Pour any remaining margarine over fish and bake at 325 degrees about 5 minutes, until fish flakes with fork. Serves 4.

*Coating mix: combine 3 parts Bisquick™ with 1 part seasoned breadcrumbs.

KEY LIME PIE*

10-inch graham cracker
  pie crust, chilled
⅔ cup fresh or
  bottled Key lime juice
½ envelope gelatin

3⅓ cups sweetened
  condensed milk
2 egg whites, stiffly beaten
1 cup heavy cream,
  beaten with ¼ cup sugar

In saucepan, heat lime juice just to boiling. Add gelatin and stir to dissolve; cool to room temperature. In bowl, combine juice with condensed milk, fold in egg whites, and pour into crust. Chill at least 6 hours. Top with sweetened whipped cream. Serves 8.

*From *Recipes and Ramblings from Glen-Ella Springs* by Barrie Aycock, copyright © 1992, Panther Creek Publishers, Turnerville, Georgia. Used by permission.

TAYLOR'S TROLLEY
Clarkesville

When Clarkesville was planned, great care was taken to site it advantageously; the main street, named for President Washington, follows a broad ridge above the Soquee River, with the courthouse on a high plateau.

Although the courthouse was demolished, the square remains the address of shops and businesses in charming old buildings.

The northeast corner block is filled by a commercial building constructed by John Martin about 1907, when it was described as "the largest and handsomest in town." Two portions of the structure were one story; the two on the south were two stories, the second floor intended for office space.

Of molded concrete block with cast-iron columns and metal cornices, the building remains in excellent condition, although the façade of the corner portion has unfortunately been bricked and altered.

The other two-story portion is remarkably well-preserved, now painted dark green and cream. Inside, many original fixtures remind the visitor that it was a drugstore for more than fifty years before becoming Taylor's Trolley restaurant in 1985.

You can still get the fountain treats you remember—ice cream cones, banana splits, lime rickeys, hand-squeezed lemonade, and genuine MILKshakes, but the rest of the Trolley's food will surprise you. Chef-owner Michael Collinson bones fresh fish and local chicken and creates his wholesome, natural food from scratch; everything is cooked to order.

At lunch, the special might be Chicken Cordon Bleu, or a salad of chicken breast over greens with an avocado vinaigrette. Baked Potatoes and burgers can be topped with a host of choices, and soups, freshly made from fresh ingredients, may be the best you've tasted.

The atmosphere is one of candlelight and flowers at dinner, when offerings change to grilled swordfish in tequila lime sauce, Duck a l'Orange, prime steaks, fresh mountain trout with pistachios, or the signature Lobster Harrington.

Unusual fresh vegetables include succotash, mushroom salad with homemade olive oil mayonnaise, or wilted greens, and desserts will take you back to your childhood.

How long since you've had old-fashioned chocolate or coconut layer cake? Perhaps you've never sampled a cake with strawberries in the batter, sour cream frosting, surrounded with strawberries. It's about time.

Taylor's Trolley, 84 Washington Street, on the square, is open Monday through Wednesday, 11 a.m. to 3:30 p.m.; Thursday through Saturday, 11 a.m. to 5 p.m., and 5 to 9 p.m. for dinner. Winter hours may vary. (706)754-5566. Dress is casual, wine and beer are available, and reservations are accepted, preferred for parties of 5 or more. AE,MC,V,Personal checks. ($$)

CORN CHOWDER

¼ cup CLARIFIED butter
½ cup diced yellow onion
⅛ cup chopped raw bacon
½ cup diced celery
Kernels from 5 ears corn,
   well scraped

¼ cup sherry
3 medium potatoes, diced
8 cups chicken stock
Pinch thyme
2 cups heavy cream
Pepper

In stockpot over low heat, sauté first 4 ingredients until tender. Add corn and cook 1 minute; add sherry and simmer 1 minute. Add potatoes, chicken stock, and thyme. Bring to boil, cook 10 minutes, remove from heat and stir in cream and pepper. Return to low heat until just hot enough to serve. Serves 10.

CRAB CAKES

1 pound lump crab meat,
   carefully picked over
1 teaspoon chopped chives
½ cup mayonnaise
2 eggs, beaten

2 Tablespoons finely chopped
   onion, lightly sautéed
½ teaspoon hot sauce
2 cups fresh bread crumbs
1 cup CLARIFIED butter

In large bowl, stir together first 6 ingredients. Slowly stir in about ½ cup bread crumbs; mixture should be fairly wet but firm enough to form patties. Cakes may be stored in refrigerator, covered, 4 days. Dredge cakes in remaining bread crumbs and sauté in butter.

LOBSTER HARRINGTON

Four 1-pound
  Maine lobsters
1 pound bay scallops
¼ cup CLARIFIED butter
4 teaspoons sherry
¼ cup sliced green olives
¼ cup sliced scallions,
  white part only
2 cups cheese/spinach
  tortellini

Juice of 1 lemon
2 cups light cream
¼ cup grated
  Parmesan cheese
¼ cup Gruyère cheese
2 dashes hot sauce
Salt and pepper
About 1 cup strong
  chicken stock
½ cup sliced
  cherry tomatoes

In large pot, cook lobsters in boiling water 10 to 12 minutes. Plunge lobsters into cold water to stop cooking. Remove tail meat and claw meat from shells; wash meat and chop coarsely. Hold shells in barely-warm oven until serving time. In large sauté pan, sauté scallops in butter over medium heat 2 to 3 minutes; be careful not to burn butter. Add next 5 ingredients and reduce heat to low. Stir in cream with cheeses and seasonings; stirring constantly, cook until cheese melts and sauce is smooth. Add stock as needed to thin sauce to creamy consistency; add tomatoes and just heat through. Divide lobster meat into shells; spoon sauce over equally. Serves 4.

THE BURNS-SUTTON HOUSE
Clarkesville

Malaria, yellow fever, and other diseases that drove Savannahians and Charlestonians to summer refuge in the North Georgia mountains were not fully understood until the Spanish-American War. Prior to nineteenth century research, swamp exhalations or "miasmas" were blamed, and people who lived in low or damp areas knew only to leave, if they were able, for higher ground.

The wealthy and prominent people who chose Clarkesville for their summer homes built handsome, comfortable houses with shady porches. Year-round residents, settlers from nearby North Carolina and Tennessee in the 1820s, later from England and Northern Europe, continued the trend. Most of their Georgia plain-style, Gothic, Georgian Revival and Queen Anne houses have porches to take advantage of the pleasant climate.

A Victorian eclectic house built in 1901 by Rush and Cornelius Church, master craftsmen, was the residence of Dr. J.K. Burns. Characterized by sweeping verandas that almost surround the first floor, it is a rambling, two-story frame structure on a pierced-brick foundation. A stained-glass window, handsome woodwork, and generous acreage indicate its importance, and that of its owner.

Dr. Burns died in 1924, and when his daughter lost her home across the street in a fire, she and her husband, Judge (previously Mayor of Clarkesville) I.H. Sutton moved in with her mother.

The house remained in the family until purchased by Habersham county for use by the Board of Education; as part of the South Washington Street Historic District, it was placed on the National Register in 1982. It had stood vacant several years when it was purchased by Jo Ann and John Smith, in 1985, and, after much effort, returned to its earlier elegance.

John, a contractor, did 95 percent of the restoration and construction of the new main dining room, which incorporates architectural fragments from several old structures: arched windows from a Louisville, Kentucky, school, French doors from Ohio, and heart-pine floors from an 1850 house in South Georgia. Jo Ann made all the new stained-glass windows.

The result is harmonious and welcoming, creating just the right atmosphere for the tasty, well-chosen food at the Burns-Sutton House.

Lunchtime brings crowds to enjoy the "hot bar," which provides two entrées and as many as six home-cooked vegetables in a hurry, with fresh hot rolls. Equally popular are quiche plates, homemade soups—tomato Florentine, California vegetable (with cream cheese), and chicken noodle—and substantial sandwiches, such as Reuben, French dip, and "Philly" cheese.

Salads include chicken, tuna, and potato, available as platters or combined; taco; and Southwestern, with kidney beans, black olives, picante sauce, sour cream and grilled chicken atop fresh greens. Many come with Jo Ann's homemade muffins—carrot spice and cran-apple are especially good.

Among desserts, pies of coconut, chocolate cream, and old-fashioned lemon meringue are choice, or choose chocolate layer cake with ice cream and hot fudge.

Friday and Saturday nights in summer, and Sunday year-round, family-style dining means all you can eat, served at the table. A typical meal might be fried chicken, barbecued beef ribs, or broiled mountain trout, with big bowls of REAL creamed potatoes, green beans, tomatoes with zucchini, and cabbage au gratin, plus homemade hot biscuits and corn bread.

If you've been wise enough to save room, you can finish with homemade peach cobbler—unless it's blackberry or apple season!

The Burns-Sutton House, 124 S. Washington Street, is ½ mile south of the square. Lunch is 11 a.m. to 3 p.m., Monday through Saturday; breakfast, Saturday and Sunday only, is 8 to 11 a.m.; Sunday family-style dining is 12N to 3 p.m. From May to December, family-style dining is available on Friday and Saturday evenings until 8 p.m. (706)754-5565. Dress is casual, reservations are accepted, and busiest time is during University of Georgia football weekends and "leaf season." There are seven overnight units. The business is occasionally closed during early January. AE,MC,V. ($$)

BROCCOLI QUICHE

9-inch unbaked pie shell
4 slices cheddar cheese
Florets from
  1 bunch broccoli
4 ounces
  grated Swiss cheese

4 eggs
2 cups half and half cream
¼ teaspoon salt
¼ teaspoon pepper
⅛ teaspoon nutmeg

Place sliced cheese on crust, top with broccoli, then grated cheese. In bowl, mix remaining ingredients; pour into crust and bake at 350 degrees about 35 minutes, or until browned and puffed.

LEMON CHESS PIE

9-inch unbaked pie shell
2 cups sugar
4 eggs

4 ounces margarine, melted
1 Tablespoon corn starch
Juice and rind of 2 lemons

In bowl, mix all ingredients well; pour into pie shell and bake at 350 degrees about 45 minutes, or until crusted and firm on top.

THE SIMMONS-BOND INN
Toccoa

A network of Indian trails across Georgia was first mapped by the British about 1715. Explorers and traders, then soldiers and settlers used these trails; some were enlarged, paved, and are still in use, frequently known by their Indian names or some Anglicization.

The important Unicoi (pronounced Ewe-na-coy) Turnpike traveled west from the Tugaloo River past Clarkesville and through the Nacoochee Valley, crossed the crest of the Blue Ridge at Unicoi Gap, then paralleled the Hiawassee River to the Overhill Cherokee towns.

In the 1870s, where the Charlotte and Atlanta Air Line Railroad terminated near the Unicoi Turnpike, the town of Toccoa was given an Indian name meaning "beautiful," the name of a nearby waterfall.

Fifteen-year-old James B. Simmons, of Clayton, went to the new town as a clerk, and prospered immediately, opening his own store at twenty-one, in 1883. As a manufacturer of kitchen cupboards, he created a substantial industry with branches in three other towns, and established and was first president of the Farmers and Merchants Bank.

Simmons hired Levi Prater, an outstanding master builder from Gainesville, to construct his house near the center of Toccoa in 1903. A two-story frame structure with a large wrap-around porch, it has elements of Queen Anne and Neoclassical styles, but is chiefly notable for spectacular oak woodwork.

Numerous Ionic columns and pilasters, extensive paneling and a double-landing staircase produce an impressive interior. With several large stained-glass windows, similar transoms in the dining room's projecting bay, and the first indoor plumbing in town, the Simmons house was hardly rivaled by the courthouse constructed across the street three years later, when Toccoa was named the seat of new Stevens County.

The house passed to the Simmons' daughter, Louise Bond, and became law offices in 1975. Placed on the National Register in 1983, it was converted to an inn in 1990 by Joni and Don Ferguson.

A popular luncheon spot for downtown workers, the Simmons-Bond Inn offers speedy service and delicious food: excellent soups (always onion, frequently seafood bisque, turkey or beef vegetable), a choice of vegetable or meat quiche, plenty of robust sandwiches, and "something special" that might be meat loaf, honey-baked chicken, pasta primavera, baked pork chops, or oriental beef over rice.

At dinner, you'll find steaks, seafood and chicken—Cordon Bleu is BROILED for health's sake—all prepared to order and accompanied by soup or salad, vegetables, and potato or rice, plus low-cal stir frys and Italian favorites such as lasagna, chicken cacciatore, or Fettuccine Alfredo.

Croutons and yeasty hot rolls are homemade, there's a fresh seafood choice, and desserts are always good. Constants are pies—chocolate walnut, delicate Key lime chiffon, traditional apple—and rich carrot cake with cream cheese icing.

The Simmons-Bond Inn, 130 West Tugalo Street, is open for lunch Monday through Saturday, 11:30 a.m. to 2 p.m., and for dinner Monday through Friday, 5 to 8 p.m. (706)886-8411; (800)533-7693. Dress is casual, beer and wine are available, and reservations are accepted but not necessary. Busiest time is "leaf season" in Autumn. There are three overnight units. AE,MC,V. ($).

CHICAGO-STYLE SHRIMP de JONGHE

½ cup bread crumbs
⅛ cup Parmesan cheese
Granulated garlic

1 Tablespoon lemon juice
4 ounces butter, melted
1 pound peeled shrimp

In small bowl, mix bread crumbs and cheese and set aside. Add garlic and lemon juice to butter and set aside. In shallow pan or oven-proof dish, place shrimp. Sprinkle with crumbs, then pour butter mixture over. Broil 3 minutes OR bake at 350 degrees 8 minutes.

CHICKEN DIJON

2 boneless chicken breasts
Butter or oil
1 teaspoon Dijon mustard
3 Tablespoons white wine
4 ounces heavy cream

Sliced mushrooms
Sliced onion
Seasoned salt and pepper
Chopped parsley for garnish

In sauté pan, sauté chicken breasts in butter or oil; when done on one side, turn over and add remaining ingredients. Simmer about 10 minutes, or until well done. Garnish with parsley and serve with seasoned rice.

BLACK RUSSIAN SANDWICH

Thinly sliced ham
Sliced turkey
Sliced Swiss cheese
Lettuce
Pumpernickel bread

Thousand Island dressing
Pickle and chips for garnish

Pile ham, turkey, cheese, and lettuce on bread. Serve open-faced, topped with dressing.

CHOCOLATE-WALNUT PIE

9-inch unbaked pie shell
1 teaspoon vanilla
3 Tablespoons butter
3 eggs, beaten
¾ cup sugar

1⅓ cups chopped walnuts
½ cup mini chocolate chips

In bowl, mix vanilla with butter and add remaining ingredients; pour into pie shell and bake at 400 degrees 10 minutes. Lower temperature to 325 degrees and bake 35 minutes. Serve warm with ice cream.

THE SOUTHERN TRACE
Lavonia

The northeastern part of Franklin County, created in 1784, was densely forested, and resisted settlement for about a hundred years, except for a few hardy pioneers who cleared land for farming. When the Elberton Air Line Railroad was completed in 1878, the town of Lavonia was laid out on both sides of the railroad in a grid, centered by the depot.

Based on agriculture—primarily cotton—and the railroad, the little community grew rapidly through the first quarter of the 20th century. Commercial buildings clustered around the depot, and residences on large lots surrounded the town, occupied by people with farms in the county.

By 1910, Lavonia had a population of some 1700 people, the city limits had been expanded twice, the depot had been relocated, and a library was under construction.

Among the many handsome residences built during the period was a two-story yellow brick in the Neoclassical style, constructed about 1918 on a large wooded lot.

The hip-roofed house has a full height pedimented entry porch supported by paired Corinthian columns; similar columns support balanced one-story porches on either side, as well as a pôrte-cochère on the right.

Despite its beauty and obvious comfort, the house has had many owners. Its builder, Charles Ray, a cotton and cattle farmer, went bankrupt in a depression that began after World War I, when cotton production declined.

Ben Cheek, the second owner, was in the insurance business and an agent for the railroad; in his later years, he went to law school, and worked as an attorney from the time he was sixty until his death. The house, sold by his sons, passed through a succession of owners, standing empty several times. As part of the Jones Street Residential Historic District, it was placed on the National Register in 1989.

The Southern Trace Inn and Restaurant since 1988, it is owned and operated by Patricia and Marvin Barnhart and their daughters. In its gracious old rooms, decorated in pale floral colors, you'll find prime rib, the "steak of the day," and fresh seafood, perhaps broiled grouper with lemon butter, or poached salmon with dill/lime mayonnaise.

The menu changes frequently, but there are often Latin and Italian specialties. Cuban Pork Sauté is served with rice and black beans, topped with chopped scallions; Barbados Chicken is enriched with black olives.

You can count on rich New York-style cheesecakes with a light crumb crust and a choice of several cold or hot toppings; and traditional blackberry cobbler, served piping hot, topped with vanilla ice cream.

The Southern Trace, 14 Baker Street at GA 17, is open for lunch Monday through Friday, 11:30 a.m. to 2 p.m., and for dinner, Monday through Saturday, 5:30 to 9 p.m. The Sunday lunch buffet is 11:30 a.m. to 2 p.m. (706)356-1033. Dress is casual, beer and wine are available (except Sunday), and reservations are requested. AE,MC,V. ($$)

FETTUCCINE À LA ASHLEY

1 pound fettuccine cooked al dente & rinsed	2 12-ounce cans evaporated milk
1 pound thick-sliced bacon, cooked, drained, and crumbled	Chopped parsley Salt and pepper Parmesan cheese
½ pound butter or margarine	3 eggs, beaten

In large, heavy skillet, melt butter over medium-low heat; place drained fettuccine in melted butter, add milk, seasonings, and cheese, and toss well to mix and coat pasta. Continuing to stir, add eggs and mix until well incorporated. Do not boil. Serve immediately, topped with crumbled bacon. Serves 6.

*Chef's note: "Be sure to have all ingredients ready, as this dish should be tossed together quickly. With a salad and crusty bread, this makes a wonderful lunch or supper meal."

HONEY-LIME CHICKEN WITH PEANUTS

3 Tablespoons butter
8 boneless, skinless chicken
  breasts, pounded lightly
Two 16-ounce cans frozen
  limeade concentrate,
  thawed

6 ounces honey
10-ounce package
  salted peanuts
Refined gravy flour
Salt
Sliced limes and chopped
  scallions for garnish

In large skillet, melt butter and sauté chicken on both sides until lightly browned. Pour limeade over chicken; pour in honey, sprinkle with peanuts, and simmer over low heat about 8 minutes, turning once. Remove breasts to warm plate. Thicken sauce with sprinkling of gravy flour, stirring constantly. Season to taste; pour sauce over chicken and garnish with scallions and sliced limes. Serves 4.

RUDOLPH'S ON GREEN STREET
Gainesville

After the Indian Cessions of 1817, Hall County was created and named for Lyman Hall, Signer of the Declaration of Independence. The county seat was laid out northwest of springs known as "Mule Camp Springs."

Gainesville's wide streets were optimistic, as few lots were taken up until gold was discovered in 1828. Then, as trading center for miners, Gainesville acquired stores, taverns, and offices. A second boom followed construction of the Charlotte and Atlanta Air Line Railroad in 1871; in 1899, Gainesville became the first town south of Baltimore with electric street lights.

Prosperous merchants and professional people chose the broad, wooded plateau above town for their impressive houses. An old stagecoach road to the springs and the mountains became Green Street, one of Northeast Georgia's outstanding neighborhoods.

Amid houses representing every architectural style, an English Tudor-style house was built on Green Street about 1915, by Annie Perry Dixon. Designed by her daughter, Mrs. John Rudolph, it was home to three generations of their family.

The house's beamed ceilings, multiple windows with stained-glass medallions, and tile fireplaces give the intended medieval feeling to a homelike dwelling. As part of the Green Street Historic District, it was placed on the National Register in 1975.

Under the expertise of Marcia Wall and Barbara Brown since 1982, Rudolph's on Green Street serves delicious Classic American Cuisine with an exciting twist: Reuben Chowder contains sauerkraut and corned beef, with rye bread croutons; lunchtime Pastry Log features a variety of fillings rolled in puff pastry; Drunken Duck is drowned in sherry, herbs, and spices; and Junk Salad combines "everything that is raw and edible."

Weekend "Chef's Dinners" are fixed-price four-course bargains, including fine wines; Sunday Brunch provides favorites and a few surprises; and special diets can be accommodated without fuss.

For dessert, choose Apple Walnut Pie with cinnamon ice cream, Amaretto Cheesecake, or huge homemade brownies with hazelnut/frangelica ice cream, whipped cream, and white chocolate frangelica sauce.

Rudolph's on Green Street, 700 Green Street, is entered from the side, and is open for lunch Monday through Friday, 11:30 a.m. until 2:30 p.m. Dinner, Monday through Thursday, is 5:30 to 10 p.m., to 11 p.m. Friday and Saturday; Sunday brunch is 11 a.m. to 2 p.m. (706)534-2226. Dress is casual, all legal beverages are available (except Sunday), and reservations are accepted. Busiest times are during Quinlan Art Show in March, local college graduations in May, "leaf season" and Gainesville's Corn Tassel Festival, 3rd week in October. AE,DS,MC,V. ($$)

BACON, LETTUCE, AND TOMATO SOUP

8 ounces bacon, diced
2 ounces margarine
11 ounces iceberg lettuce,
 in julienne
5 ounces flour

Chicken granules
½ pound tomatoes, diced
Pinch nutmeg
Dash ground red pepper
2 cups half and half cream
Buttered croutons for garnish

In stockpot, cook bacon until lightly browned; leave in pot with fat, and add margarine. Heat until melted; stir in lettuce and sauté 2 minutes. Add flour and stir 3 minutes, or until evenly cooked. Remove from heat and stir in 7 cups hot water and chicken granules to taste. Add tomatoes and seasonings and heat to boiling; lower heat and cook 6 minutes, stirring occasionally. Mix in cream and heat to simmer, stirring frequently. Serves 10.

SCALLOPS EN PAPILLOTE

For each serving:
5 ounces sea scallops
2 asparagus spears, in thirds
3 mushrooms, halved
3 strips sweet red pepper

3 strips sweet yellow pepper,
 optional
3 strips carrot
4 scallions, in 2" strips
Court Bouillon*

Wrap scallops and vegetables in foil, leaving opening to ladle in 3 ounces court bouillon;* seal tightly, and bake at 350 degrees 15 minutes. Open carefully—steam will escape.

*Court Bouillon: in stockpot, combine 14 cups water, 2 cups white wine, 3 ounces diced onion, 2 ounces diced celery, 2⅓ ounces diced carrot, 1 teaspoon peppercorns, 5 sprigs parsley, 1 bay leaf, and ½ lemon, sliced thin. Bring to boil, reduce heat, and simmer ½ hour. Strain. Keep on hand for poaching fish or chicken.

PUMPKIN CHEESECAKE

Almond/crumb crust*
1½ pounds cream cheese
2½ cups sugar
¼ cup vanilla
5 eggs, beaten
1½ pounds
  cooked pumpkin

2 cups half and half cream
½ ounce cinnamon
½ teaspoon ginger
½ teaspoon nutmeg
Whipped cream and
  nutmeg for garnish

In large bowl of mixer, beat cheese and add remaining ingredients; pour into prepared crust. Place pan in larger pan with 1" water; bake at 300 degrees 3 hours. When chilled, slice with thin, warm knife; serve with whipped cream dusted with nutmeg.

*Crust: in large bowl, mix 1 cup graham cracker crumbs, 8 ounces crushed almonds, 3 ounces melted butter, and ¼ teaspoon almond extract. Pat firmly into bottom of 10" springform pan; bake at 350 degrees 10 minutes.

TRUMPS AT THE GEORGIAN
Athens

Chartered in 1785, the University of Georgia actually began in 1801, when John Milledge, later Governor, donated 633 acres overlooking the Oconee River for the school and a town.

Classes were held outdoors until the first permanent building was completed in 1805; "Old College" still stands.

Juxtaposition of town and gown benefited both; Athens became the commercial center of Northeast Georgia, and the college was a true university by the first quarter of the 20th century.

Although visitors to the University and business travelers stayed at a number of small hotels, by 1908, Athens, with a population of 10,000, needed a new hotel.

At a cost of $200,000, the impressive 5-story brick Georgian Hotel was constructed on the highest ridge in Clarke County, and boasted a marble lobby, stained glass windows and skylights, and running water in every room. For generations, it hosted social, business, and political functions; as part of the Downtown Historic District, it was placed on the National Register in 1978.

The hotel ceased operation in 1976; in 1985, it was rehabilitated as an apartment building, and in 1987, Helene and Ron Schwartz and Andrée Kosak moved their successful restaurant, Trumps, into the marble lobby.

At lunch and Sunday Brunch, light streams through stained glass in shades of cream, green and rose, creating an atmosphere of cheerful elegance; in the evening, candlelight enhances carefully set tables and Trumps' "good, fresh food" prepared to order in a contemporary Continental manner.

Fresh ingredients are treated with a light touch and combined with flair. Seared salmon might appear in Bloody Mary sauce, or sautéed grouper with soft shell crab and two sauces—and great pride is taken in their special beef dishes, including a huge Kansas City strip. There's always at least one vegetarian item, and special diets are accommodated.

Trumps' most popular desserts are cheesecakes—Kahlúa almond chocolate chip, for one—and such delights as homemade carrot cake with cream cheese frosting and pecans, and sinfully rich Key lime pie.

Trumps at The Georgian, 247 East Washington Street, is open for lunch Monday through Friday, 11 a.m. to 2:30 p.m., for dinner Monday through Thursday, 5 to 10 p.m., until 11 Friday and Saturday. Sunday brunch is 10:30 a.m. to 2 p.m. (706)546-6388. All legal beverages are served, dress is "casual and up," and reservations are suggested. Additional rooms are available for larger groups booked in advance. Busiest times are University of Georgia graduation and football weekends. AE,MC,V. ($$)

SPINACH AND FETA CHEESE IN PHYLLO PASTRY

3-pound package
  frozen spinach, thawed
1 bunch scallions, chopped
1½ cups crumbled feta cheese
2 Tablespoons chopped garlic

6 eggs, beaten
2½ teaspoons white pepper
1-pound package
  phyllo pastry, thawed
½ cup CLARIFIED butter

Squeeze excess liquid from spinach by hand. Add next 5 ingredients and mix well. Keeping remaining sheets covered, carefully lay out 1 sheet phyllo, brush with butter, top with 2nd sheet. Place spinach mixture along long edge of phyllo and roll up, sealing with butter. Repeat; recipe makes 6 or 8 long rolls. Separate rolls with waxed paper and freeze; cut, frozen, into 1" pieces and bake at 350 degrees 35 minutes or until golden brown. Yields about 60 appetizers.

CRÊPES SAN LUIS

8 prepared crêpes
Butter
½ cup chopped onion
¼ cup chopped green pepper
¼ cup chopped celery
2 teaspoons minced garlic
¼ cup sherry wine
½ cup diced tomato
½ pound sea scallops

½ pound small shrimp,
  shelled
¼ pound crab meat
½ pound white fish,
  in chunks
½ cup heavy cream
½ teaspoon cumin
½ teaspoon tumeric
Pinch dried basil
Salt and pepper

In large hot sauté pan, melt butter and sauté onion and pepper 2 minutes. Add next 8 ingredients and simmer 3 to 5 minutes, until shrimp is cooked through. Add cream and seasonings and blend well. Divide into 8 crêpes; roll, brush lightly with oil, and bake at 325 degrees 5 minutes. Serve with fresh salsa, sour cream, and chopped scallions. Serves 4.

CHOCOLATE CHIP PECAN PIE

9-inch unbaked pie shell
Semi-sweet chocolate chips
   to cover bottom of shell
¾ cup chopped pecans
2 Tablespoons bourbon

5 eggs, beaten
1¼ cups sugar
⅝ cup corn syrup
¼ teaspoon salt
¼ teaspoon vanilla
4 Tablespoons butter

Pierce pastry with fork and sprinkle in chips. In bowl, mix pecans and bourbon. In another bowl, beat next 6 ingredients; add drained pecans. Pour mixture into shell, place pie on paper-lined baking sheet, and bake at 375 degrees exactly one hour. Serve at room temperature or slightly warm with ice cream.

HARRY BISSETT'S
NEW ORLEANS CAFÉ AND OYSTER BAR
Athens

From its inception, Athens was destined to be a center of learning and culture. The committee that chose the site of Franklin College (later the University of Georgia) at Cedar Shoals on the Oconee River, named the town before it existed.

When it was laid out in 1801, Athens was a small grid of a few streets, but by 1829, it had a population of 1300, and proclaimed that it was no longer a village, but a town.

Across Front Street (later Broad) from the University were stores and banks; establishments selling spiritous liquors were banned by law.

By the early 1900s, "Bankers Row" on Broad Street included The National Bank of Athens on the corner of Jackson Street, The Athens Savings Bank, and, farthest west, the American State Bank. The least ornate of the three, a two-story yellow brick and stone structure with a columned first-floor facade, it was constructed before 1890 as Dr. R. M. Smith's Drug Store.

As part of the Downtown Historic District, it was placed on the National Register in 1978, and in 1986, it became Harry Bissett's New Orleans Café. Earlier restoration had installed tin ceilings made from old molds and electrified gaslights, and had enclosed the open space behind the building with a glass roof.

Harry Bissett's gave the building true New Orleans charm, establishing a comfortable atmosphere in the Oyster Bar that contrasts with the openness of the soaring courtyard. Upstairs, in the bank's former board room, there is a more formal feeling, but wherever you dine, you'll find the same attention to detail, enticing, succulent food, and attentive service.

The New Orleans flavor is enhanced by gumbo, several types of jambalaya, étouffées, blackened specialties, and fresh seafoods. Lunchtime sandwiches include po' boys of oysters, shrimp, and soft shell crab, plus a "Cajunburger," and a "Garden District" salad.

In the evenings, you'll find the Créole appetizers you'd expect—Oysters Bienville and Rockefeller, Shrimp Rémoulade, and "Cajun Popcorn" of fried crawfish tails, as well as a host of entrées and a greater choice of good vegetables than anywhere you can name.

Between meals, the Bar Menu provides sandwiches, soups, appetizers, lots of oysters, and all the famous New Orleans beverages, plus one you'll find nowhere but Athens, Georgia: the "Hair O' The Dawg Bloody Mary."

Harry Bissett's New Orleans Café and Oyster Bar, 279 E. Broad Street, is open for lunch Monday through Saturday, 11:30 a.m. to 3 p.m. Dinner, Monday through Thursday, is 5:30 to 10 p.m., until 11 p.m. Friday and Saturday. (706)353-7065. Dress is casual, all legal beverages are available, and reservations are preferred. Busiest times are University of Georgia football weekends, and Mardi Gras week. AE,MC,V. ($$)

POTATO AND TASSO SOUP

1 cup flour
1 cup vegetable oil
1 cup chopped onion
½ teaspoon chopped garlic
½ pound chopped tasso
   (spicy Cajun smoked ham)*
1 quart rich beef stock

1 Tablespoon cayenne
1 Tablespoon pepper
½ teaspoon filé powder
Salt
12-ounce can tomato pieces
3 baking potatoes,
   peeled and cubed
Chopped scallions for garnish

In 2-quart pot, cook flour and oil over medium heat, whisking constantly, until dark roux forms. To stop browning, add onion. Lower heat, add garlic and tasso, and sauté 2 minutes. Add remaining ingredients, bring to boil, and simmer, covered, 1 hour. Garnish with scallions. Yields about 6 8-ounce servings.

*Any good quality smoked sausage may be substituted, but spices may need adjusting.

MAQUE CHOUX
(pronounced "mock shoe")

8 ears yellow corn
½ pound butter
1 cup chopped onion

1 cup chopped green pepper
½ teaspoon pepper
¼ cup white wine
12-ounce can tomato pieces

Slit corn kernels in half lengthwise; cut from cob, scraping cob to retain the milk. In 2-quart pot, melt butter over medium heat. Stir in onion and pepper and sauté until translucent. Add remaining ingredients, cover, and simmer 20 minutes.

CRAWFISH ÉTOUFFÉE

½ pound butter
1 cup chopped onion
½ cup chopped
  green pepper
½ cup flour
¼ cup chopped parsley
½ cup chopped scallions,
  divided

2 teaspoons cayenne
1 teaspoon pepper
1 teaspoon thyme
Salt
1½ cups fish stock
1½ pounds crawfish
  tail meat with fat*
Juice of ½ lemon

In large skillet, melt butter over medium heat. Sauté onion and green pepper until translucent. Stir in flour, mixing until smooth. Add parsley and half the scallions; mix thoroughly. Add spices and stock; cook 5 minutes. Stir in crawfish; cook 10 minutes. Just before serving, stir in lemon juice. Serve over cooked rice and garnish with remaining scallions.

*Crawfish tails are available in 1-pound packets at gourmet stores and seafood houses. Orange color indicates fat, which carries the distinctive crawfish flavor.

ANOTHER THYME
Washington

Wilkes County, one of Georgia's original eight counties, was created by the Constitution of 1777 out of the "New Purchase," of 1773 Indian cessions. For many years Georgia's largest county, Wilkes had more than one-third of the state's population in the 1790 census.

Washington, its seat, was one of the first towns laid out after Independence, on a site near the Revolutionary battle of Kettle Creek, in which the British invasion of Georgia was halted.

On its Public Square was a popular stagecoach inn; many travelers, particularly those from Virginia and North Carolina, settled in Washington, which soon boasted business establishments around the Market Square.

A fire in 1841 destroyed the entire west side of the Square, and in 1895, the same area was hit by a fire which started in the cellar of a frame building owned by the Fitzpatrick estate. Ultimately 25 buildings were consumed, and the courthouse was damaged by smoke; when the section was rebuilt the second time, great care was taken to use "fireproof" materials.

Dominating the block is the massive Fitzpatrick Hotel, a fanciful brick and stone structure of three stories with elements of Richardsonian Romanesque design, built in 1898. Stepped Dutch gables over protruding bays center the front, and a round turret on the southern corner is crowned with a bell-shaped dome. It was placed on the National Register in 1982.

After being closed for thirty years, the hotel was purchased by Pam and Rodney Eaton, who have renovated the first floor for its original use as retail space. Restoration of upper floors is proceeding gradually.

In the hotel's long, narrow lobby and former public rooms, the Another Thyme restaurant, operated by Marsha and Lee Campbell and their daughters, offers tasty, attractive food created in its tiny, visible kitchen.

Homemade soups—cheddar cheese, vegetable, French onion (full of Provolone cheese) and Prime Rib Bisque, made with their famous marinated steak—are a good beginning. For lunch, you might follow with a hot entrée, a sandwich on homemade bread, or a special salad with homemade dressing.

In the evening, "P.M. Platters" are added, including homemade yeast rolls with such entrees as baked marinated chicken, barbecued pork, turkey/cheese quiche, and a 12-ounce marinated steak.

Desserts, homemade, of course, are known far and wide. Carrot cake with cream cheese icing is most popular, but short-crust fudge pie with pecans, Kahlúa Brownies, and pecan-crust cheesecake are hard to turn down. Newest and gooiest is the Fudge Praline Delight: don't miss it!

Another Thyme, 18 West Public Square, is open for lunch Monday through Friday 9 a.m. to 2 p.m., and Saturday, 11 a.m. to 2 p.m. Dinner, Thursday through Saturday, is 6 to 8:30 p.m. (706)678-1672. Dress is "tasteful casual," reservations are requested for parties of 12 or more, and busiest time is during house tours in April of odd-numbered years. No credit cards accepted; personal checks accepted. ($)

ANOTHER THYME SLAW

1 Tablespoon milk
2 or 3 Tablespoons mustard
2 heaping Tablespoons
 mayonnaise

½ cup sugar
1½ cups grated cabbage
¼ cup grated carrot

In bowl, whisk first four ingredients until well blended. Stir in cabbage and carrot and refrigerate. Serves 4.

BANANA BREAD

½ cup butter
3 bananas, mashed
1 cup sugar
3 eggs

Pinch of salt
1 teaspoon baking soda
1½ cups flour

In large bowl, cream butter, add bananas, sugar, and eggs and mix thoroughly. Stir in dry ingredients. Pour into greased loaf pan and bake at 350 degrees about 45 minutes or until firm but not dry.

FUDGE PRALINE DELIGHT

2½ cups flour
1½ cups sugar
4 Tablespoons cocoa
3 teaspoons baking powder
1 teaspoon salt
1 cup milk
4 tablespoons
   melted margarine

2 teaspoons vanilla
2 cups sugar
2 teaspoons cocoa
Dash salt
Pralines,* vanilla ice cream
   and butter-flavored syrup

In large bowl, combine flour with next four ingredients; blend in milk, margarine and vanilla, and spread in ungreased 9" x 13" pan. In small bowl, combine sugar, cocoa, and salt; sprinkle over cake batter. Pour 2⅔ cups hot water over cake, and bake at 350 degrees 35 to 45 minutes, or until center is firm. Cut into 12 squares. To assemble, place warm cake square on plate, top with 2 scoops ice cream, crumble pralines on top, and drizzle with syrup. Serves 12.

*Pralines: in deep, heavy saucepan, mix 2 cups sugar, 1 cup milk, and 4 teaspoons baking soda; bring to boil, and add 2 Tablespoons butter. Cook to soft ball stage. Remove from heat, add 2 cups chopped pecans, and beat until mixture loses its transparency. Drop spoonfuls onto waxed paper. A delicious candy!

THE ADAIRSVILLE INN
RESTAURANT
Adairsville

The Western and Atlantic Railroad was created by the Georgia Legislature in 1836 to run between Chattanooga and the Chattahoochee. At the line's mid-point in the fertile Oothcalooga valley, machine shops were built to serve the railroad, and in 1836, the little settlement of Adairsville relocated to the railroad line.

Named for Cherokee Chief John Adair, the town was incorporated in 1854, a milling center for the wheat farms of the valley. The largest mill belonged to J.M. Veach, a town founder.

Adairsville was not completely destroyed during the War Between the States, although there was a battle just north of town, and the "Great Locomotive Chase" took place in the area. The entire town, 185 buildings on some 170 acres, was placed on the National Register in 1987.

A grandson and namesake of mill owner/merchant Veach built a frame bungalow on South Main in the late 1920s; when his widow moved to Atlanta, several acres were purchased by the Methodist church next door. After brief use as a community lodge, the house was sold to Jim and Sharon Southerland for use as a restaurant.

Entered through a rear addition, The Adairsville Inn is bright and open, with seating in several original rooms and a new dining room, from which frequent trains may be seen through large picture windows.

Visitors gather at lunch to enjoy Sharon's crêpes filled with ham and broccoli, seafood, or chicken and mushrooms—or strawberries, for dessert—Jim's Hot Brown or other substantial sandwiches, or the Daily Special, which could be anything from quiche to Chicken Piccata to Beef Stroganoff over noodles.

In the evening, steaks, fish, and other seafoods are popular, but the Inn's all-the-time homemade favorites are wonderful breads, rich soups filled with heavy cream and fresh ingredients, and Sharon's utterly incredible desserts.

The Adairsville Inn, 100 S. Main Street, is about 1 mile from I-75 via exit 128. Westbound on GA 140, cross US 41, and take next left. It is open 7 days a week; lunch is 11 a.m. to 2 p.m., Monday through Saturday, 11:30 a.m. to 2 p.m. Sunday. Dinner, Thursday through Saturday, is 5 to 9 p.m. It is closed between Christmas and New Years', and a few days around July 4. (706)773-2774. Dress is "jeans to fur coats," reservations are accepted only for parties of 8 or more, and credit cards are not accepted; personal checks accepted. ($$)

LEMON CHICKEN

1 cup flour
2 Tablespoons lemon &
  pepper seasoning salt
8 boneless chicken breasts
½ cup butter

¼ cup oil
Juice of 2 lemons
8 slices lemon
½ to 1 cup dry white wine
Fresh parsley

Mix flour with salt and dredge chicken. In skillet, melt butter with oil and sauté chicken. Transfer cooked breasts to platter, sprinkle with lemon juice, and keep warm. In same pan, sauté lemon slices 3 minutes or until transparent. Place one lemon slice on each breast. Add wine to pan; reduce until slightly thickened. Spoon over breasts and serve. Garnish with parsley. Serves 8.

CHOCOLATE ESPRESSO TORTE

1 pound butter, cubed
1 cup + 2 Tablespoons sugar
1 cup + 2 Tablespoons
  hot espresso coffee
1 pound bittersweet or semi-
  sweet chocolate, chopped

6 large eggs, beaten
  with 6 large egg yolks
Powdered sugar
Whipped cream
Chocolate shavings

Line buttered 8" springform pan with waxed paper, then butter and flour paper. In large heavy pan, stir butter, sugar, and coffee over medium-low heat until dissolved. Add chocolate and stir smooth; remove from heat. Whisk in room-temperature eggs, and pour into prepared pan. Place pan on baking sheet and bake at 325 degrees about 1 hour or until edges crack, but center is not completely set. Do not overbake; cake sets as it cools. Cool on rack, then cover and refrigerate overnight. Run knife around edges; carefully release pan. Sift on powdered sugar. Cut into wedges, cleaning knife each time. Serve topped with whipped cream and chocolate shavings. Serves 16.

PECAN DELIGHT

¾ cup unsalted butter,
   softened
½ cup sugar
1 egg
2¼ cups flour

1½ cups light brown sugar,
   packed
1 cup unsalted butter
½ cup honey
1 pound pecans
¼ cup heavy cream

In large bowl of mixer, cream butter and sugar; beat in egg. Add flour and just combine; gather dough into ball, flatten, cover, and chill 30 minutes. Line 9" x 13" pan with waxed paper. Roll out dough between waxed paper to ¼" thick rectangle; transfer dough to prepared pan. Trim edges and refrigerate while making filling. In large heavy pan over low heat, melt sugar, butter, and honey. Bring to boil and stir in pecans and cream: mixture will bubble. Immediately spread mixture over pastry and bake at 375 degrees about 25 minutes or until filling bubbles and is deep golden brown. Do not overcook! Run knife between crust and pan. Cool completely, invert onto another pan, then right side up. Cut into 2" squares and serve with vanilla ice cream, if desired. Store remainder in airtight container. Serves 24.

TIBERIO RESTAURANT
Rome

Prehistoric Indians built a large town near the point where the Oostanaula and Etowah rivers flow together to become the Coosa; later, the area was the last foothold of the Cherokee in Georgia until they were dispossessed in the 1830s.

In 1834, four investors determined to build a town at the confluence, and to have the county seat moved to the new location, which they found eminently suitable for commerce. Land was purchased, ferries and bridges were planned, and the town was laid out in a grid between the rivers. Rome, like its namesake, was built on seven hills.

During the War Between the States, Rome's large foundry, which supplied cannon to the Confederacy, became a Union target. The town was finally occupied in 1864 by Union forces, who burned it as they evacuated.

Rome rebuilt during the 1870s and '80s. About 1890, a striking brick and stone commercial building, with corner entrance and elements of Richardsonian Romanesque style, was erected at Broad and Second for Bass and Heard's department and farmers' supply store. By 1910, it was the new home of the First National Bank; the entrance was moved to the Broad Street façade and the first floor raised due to frequent high water.

After a later occupant, The Trust Company Bank, relocated, the building stood vacant for 20 years. As part of the Between the Rivers Historic District, it was placed on the National Register in 1983.

Piero Barba, a native of Italy, had been successful in the insurance business in Rome for sixteen years, but longed for a restaurant. In 1988, he sold his insurance agency, put together a company, and negotiated a lease on the former bank building. After six months of renovation, during which the eighteen-ton vault door was removed, Tiberio Restaurant was opened on June 1, 1989.

Utilizing the classic elements in the bank—fluted square columns, high ceilings, marble floors, and tall windows—Tiberio creates the magic of Capri (Emperor Tiberio's last home) in an excellent adaptive use.

The daily lunch buffet, in a well-designed addition, is quick and reasonable; monthly Sunday brunch buffets are lavish, with six entrées, four or five pastas, and six or eight vegetables; and you can eat in the courtyard in fine weather from a separate light menu.

Prime veal might be served with a lemon butter sauce, or sautéed with capers in a white wine-black olive sauce with roasted pimientos. Salmon is sautéed with pesto, and grouper with spinach, and grilled filet of beef is topped with shrimp, mushrooms, and fresh tomatoes.

For dessert, keep in mind Chocolate Mousse Cake, with a vodka-scented mousse between layers of chocolate cake, topped with shaved chocolate.

Whatever your choice, at Tiberio, surrounded by comfortable elegance, you'll enjoy extraordinary Regional Italian Cuisine, with the freshest ingredients expertly prepared and graciously served.

Tiberio Restaurant, 201 Broad Street, is open for lunch Monday through Friday, 11 a.m. to 2 p.m., for dinner Monday through Thursday, 6 to 9:30 p.m., Friday and Saturday to 10 p.m. Sunday brunch buffet is the last Sunday in each month. (706)291-2229. All legal beverages are available, dress is "casually elegant" (most men wear coats and ties at dinner), and reservations are accepted, advisable on weekends. Busiest times are Monday evening and Friday lunch. AE,DC,MC,V. ($$)

BUTTERNUT SQUASH SOUP
WITH APPLE PURÉE

2 pounds peeled, de-seeded
  butternut squash
2 pounds peeled, cored,
  chopped apples
2 cups chopped onion
4 slices white bread
2 quarts chicken broth

2¾ teaspoon salt (or to taste)
2½ teaspoons EACH
  rosemary, oregano,
  white pepper
8 large egg yolks
2 cups + 1 ounce heavy cream

In stockpot, combine first five ingredients and all seasonings; cook until squash is done. Purée in batches in blender or food processor; return to pot. Mix yolks and cream, add to soup, and heat to simmer. Serves 16.

CAPELLE D'ANGELO

1 pound dry angel hair
  pasta, cooked al dente
4 Tablespoons
  extra virgin olive oil
8 cloves garlic, sliced thin
8 ounces tomato, diced

12 leaves fresh basil,
  in julienne
1 ounce veal or
  chicken stock
4 pinches mixed salt
  and white pepper
Basil or cilantro for garnish

In sauté pan, heat oil and cook garlic over low heat to golden brown. Add remaining ingredients and sauté briefly. Toss with cooked pasta; garnish with fresh basil leaf or chopped cilantro.

PESTO SAUCE

Handful of pine nuts
30 leaves fresh basil
2 cloves garlic

Pinch salt
1 Tablespoon
  Parmesan cheese
½ cup extra virgin olive oil

In blender or food processor, combine all ingredients and blend. Serve tossed with cooked pasta, hot or cold, on grilled fish, or added to soup.

Chef's note: this is particularly good for flavoring minestrone.

THE LICKSKILLET FARM RESTAURANT

North Roswell, near Alpharetta

In the summer of 1864, in preparation for a battle that never took place, Confederates dug trenches on the Miller's cotton farm, in what is now North Fulton County, about two miles east of Alpharetta.

There were skirmishes in the area, however, and sniper fire; according to legend, a slave discovered a dead Union soldier in the stream near the trenches, and named it "Foekiller Creek."

The farmhouse, built in 1846, was bought and enlarged about 1960 by two enterprising women who operated a popular restaurant and antiques shop.

Sophisticated country charm, as typified by 1940s movies about Connecticut, appealed to diners for more than thirty years; the peaceful, wooded terrain provided a delightful contrast to nearby urban sprawl, and the food was renowned.

A good deal of repair was needed by the time Mickey and Donna Brock bought it in 1991; Donna's decorating skill has brightened the interior with yellow trim, fruit-patterned curtains, and apple-green chairs painted with fruit.

As soon as you are seated you'll be brought a skillet of tasty, warm corn bread, indicative of Lickskillet Farm's hospitality. Dinners include soup, salad, two vegetables, and hot rolls—you can't leave hungry—and you can choose from such fare as Scallops Evonne, with a vegetable salsa; the Carpetbagger (stuffed with shrimp and sautéed crab); or Halibut Your Way (grilled, broiled, or blackened, with Maître D' Butter).

The famous Sunday Brunch Buffet might include pork chops, country ham, eggs, spiced apples, asparagus vinaigrette, and other breakfast items, served with champagne.

In pleasant weather, you can feast on the deck or in the gazebo, then examine the well-preserved trenches to work off your calories.

Lickskillet Farm Restaurant is at 1380 OLD Roswell Road, 1.3 miles north of Holcomb Bridge Road, at the corner of Rockmill Road. It is open for lunch, Monday through Friday, 11:15 a.m. to 2:15 p.m. Dinner, Monday through Saturday, begins at 6:30 p.m., with the last reservation taken at 10 p.m. Sunday brunch buffet is 10:30 a.m. to 2:30 p.m. (404)475-6484. Dress is casual, although most men wear coat and tie, all legal beverages are available, and reservations are requested. Busiest times are the Thanksgiving Feast, when seatings are every 2 hours from 11:30 a.m., with the last seating at 4:30 p.m., and Valentine's Day. AE,DS,MC,V. ($$$)

LICKSKILLET FARM'S FAMOUS CORN BREAD

4 eggs
2 cups sour cream
1½ cups cream-style corn

½ cup cracklings*
2 Tablespoons sugar
2 cups corn meal
½ cup salad oil

Oil two 8" cast iron skillets. In large bowl, combine ingredients in order, blending carefully after sugar, then after oil. Divide mixture between pans, and bake at 400 degrees 25 minutes, or until golden brown. Serve warm.

*Cracklings are fat pork from which the fat has been rendered. They have a gentle crunch and a sweet, nutty flavor; there is no substitute, although they may be omitted.

VEAL CABRIOLET

24-ounce veal strip loin,
  in 8 equal portions
8 Tablespoons butter

8 tomatoes, cored and peeled
12 scallions, chopped
8 ounces feta cheese
Additional feta cheese

Grill veal until rare. In large hot sauté pan, melt butter and add tomatoes, scallions, and cheese; cook over medium-low heat until cheese melts. Add veal to mixture and raise heat; if sauce gets too hot, it will break. Place 2 slices veal on each plate, top with sauce, and crumble cheese on top. Serves 4.

STEAK AU POIVRE

Two 12-ounce
  New York strip steaks
½ cup crushed peppercorns
2 ounces olive oil

1 cup Bordeaux wine
2 cups demi-glace or
  rich brown gravy
Additional peppercorns

Remove all fat from steaks. Place pepper on each side of steaks and pound with meat tenderizer until ingrained in the beef. In large skillet, heat oil, and sear steaks on both sides until oil is smoking. Add half the wine—be prepared for a flame—let flame burn out, and add demi-glace and remaining wine. Let sauce thicken. Remove from heat, place steak on plate, and ladle sauce over. Garnish with peppercorns. Serves 2.

SAUTÉED FROG LEGS

6 or 8 pairs frog legs
1 cup flour
3 Tablespoons olive oil
2 Tablespoons
  chopped scallions
2 Tablespoons
  crushed garlic

½ cup Marsala wine
1 cup brown sauce or
  rich brown gravy
2 teaspoons lemon juice
Additional chopped
  scallions

In bowl, coat frog legs with flour; shake off excess. In skillet, heat oil, add legs to pan, and sauté golden brown. Add next four ingredients and heat through; be careful not to overcook frog legs as they will get very tough. Add lemon juice. Serve frog legs topped with sauce and garnished with scallions. Serves 3 or 4.

VILLA D' ESTE
(formerly La Grotta)
Roswell

Roswell King, of Darien, near Savannah, selected a town site on the Chattahoochee River in 1829, and bought a large tract of land. Visualizing a town similar to those in New England, centered around a square, in 1837, he and his son, Barrington, relocated and built a cotton mill, one of the earliest industries in North Georgia.

By offering acreage to any friend who would settle there, they soon established a town, which was incorporated in 1854 and named for Mr. King.

Roswell was home to many wealthy people, and the town's early residential section is characterized by their fine Greek Revival houses; one of these, Bulloch Hall, was the childhood home of Mittie Bulloch, mother of President Theodore Roosevelt and grandmother of Eleanor Roosevelt.

Over-farmed cotton land caused a depression in the mid-nineteenth century, and Roswell, further damaged by Union occupation and vandalism during the War Between the States, was slow to recover. The mill, burned by Federals, was rebuilt, but the town never regained its industrial prominence.

Prior to 1874, a hip-roofed frame cottage was built north of Roswell's public square for a Dr. Grier; according to local tradition, it was constructed by three brothers who owed him money. He lived and practiced medicine there until his death, stabling his horses in the basement. As part of the Roswell Historic District, it was placed on the National Register in 1974.

The house was chosen as a second location for Atlanta's successful La Grotta restaurant in 1981; in 1992, Gildo Fusinaz, one of the partners, became sole proprietor, changing the name to avoid confusion.

Decorated in shades of rose and peach, with enclosed porches overlooking a 150-year-old tree, Villa D'Este specializes in Northern Italian cuisine, with fresh pastas and rich cream sauces, and the finest ingredients are prepared to order in traditional recipes with a modern flair.

Especially popular here are veal dishes; notable are grilled veal chop with sun-dried tomatoes, blanched garlic and parsley butter, and Veal Florentine, topped with sautéed spinach, Mozarella, and a light cream sauce.

Nightly seafood specials present the market's freshest, combining, for instance, shrimp with olives, or baby salmon with lemon butter. Other unusual combinations include pork tenderloin filet stuffed with spinach and pineapple, topped with a Dijon mustard sauce.

From soups—tortellini in chicken and beef broth, cream of fennel, cream of asparagus—to desserts—velvety Crème Caramel; Tira Misù; and trifle with kiwi, strawberries, and peaches, soaked in amaretto and coffee liqueurs—you'll experience an outstanding meal.

Villa D'Este, 647 Atlanta Street, is just north of the square, and is open Tuesday through Saturday, 6 to 10:30 p.m.; weekend seatings are at 7 and 9 p.m. (404)998-0645. Dress is "smart casual," all legal beverages are served, and reservations are advisable. It is closed the week of July 4 and the following week. AE,DC,DS,MC,V. ($$$)

CALAMARI SALAD

1¼ pounds cleaned squid
6 ounces olive oil, divided
½ medium red onion,
 thinly sliced
1 cup sliced
 Shiitake mushrooms
½ teaspoon minced garlic

1 sweet red pepper, roasted,
 peeled, in julienne
2 ounces tomato juice
3 ounces red wine vinegar
¼ cup fresh basil,
 in julienne
Salt and pepper

In large stockpot, bring ½ gallon lightly salted water to a boil. Place squid in water and cook 3 to 4 minutes, or until done. Drain, cut into strips and set aside. In sauté pan in 2 ounces olive oil, sauté onion, mushrooms, and garlic. In large bowl, combine all ingredients and season to taste.

THE PUBLIC HOUSE
ON ROSWELL SQUARE
Roswell

An enlightened industrialist for his day, Roswell King had his cotton mill in operation by 1839, and that year constructed the "Old Bricks," the first apartments built in the South, for millworkers. Within twenty years, the town could boast two cotton mills, a woolen mill, flour mill, and a tannery, employing 250 workers.

Cotton and woolen fabrics supplied to the Confederacy by the mills made them prime targets of the Union Army. After the occupation of Marietta, Garrard's Cavalry was sent to take Roswell and guard the Chattahoochee bridge. On July 5, 1864, he reported having burned cotton mills, woolen mill, paper mills, flouring mills, and machine shops. The bridge had been burned by Johnston's retreating army.

In one of the most heartless and senseless acts of the war, the women millworkers were deported, often with only the clothes they were wearing, and after watching their homes burned; some were forced to leave their children behind. Filling a hundred and ten army wagons, they were hauled to Marietta and boarded onto two entire north-bound trains with supplies for nine days. On Sherman's orders, they were "set adrift in Indiana," and few, if any, ever saw their families again.

Despite destruction and later damage from Union troops, hospitalized soldiers, and refugees, much of Roswell remains unchanged, and the Roswell Historic District was placed on the National Register in 1974.

In the Greek Revival company store of Roswell Manufacturing Company, built in 1854, an enduring and popular restaurant has been operated by the Peasant group since 1976. The two-story Public House has high ceilings, exposed brick walls, original floors, and lots of soft touches—white tablecloths, fresh flowers, oil paintings, antique platters—and great food.

"Creative American Cuisine" here means Rosemary Lemon Rack of Lamb, Wild Mushroom Chicken, Salmon in a Cornhusk, and Steak au Poivre. It means your soup might be red pepper, tomato basil, or corn and shrimp chowder, and your dessert will be HUGE; many people split one.

If you have to ask a stranger to share, don't miss Frozen Caramel Mousse: vanilla mousse layered with chocolate, caramel, and Heath Bars, topped with chocolate sauce, whipped cream, and MORE crushed Heath Bars.

The Public House on Roswell Square, 605 Atlanta Street, is open 7 days a week. Lunch, Monday through Friday, is 11:30 a.m. to 3:30 p.m., until 3 p.m. Saturday and Sunday. Dinner, Sunday through Thursday, is 5:30 to 10 p.m., until 11 p.m Friday and Saturday. (404)992-4646. Dress is casual, all legal beverages are available, and reservations are accepted only for groups of 8 or more, early in the evening. AE,CB,DC,MC,V. ($$)

MARINATED CHICKEN LIVERS

2 Tablespoons cider vinegar	½ cup flour
2 Tablespoons lemon juice	1½ teaspoons salt
1 teaspoon garlic salt	½ teaspoon pepper
½ teaspoon white pepper	2 pounds chicken livers
½ teaspoon dry mustard	About 2 Tablespoons oil
1 cup vegetable oil	2 green peppers, in julienne
	Cherry tomatoes

In blender, combine first 5 ingredients; gradually add oil, blending smooth. Refrigerate marinade. In shallow pan, mix flour with seasonings; dredge livers in flour. In skillet over medium heat, sauté livers in oil a few at a time until stiffened; turn over and cook 2 minutes or until firm but still pink inside. Add peppers and marinate in dressing several hours or overnight. To serve, place livers on leaf lettuce and garnish with cherry tomatoes.

SALAD DRESSING

¾ cup soy sauce	1 teaspoon toasted
3 Tablespoons lemon juice	sesame seeds
1 teaspoon sugar	1 teaspoon chopped onion
	1¼ cups peanut oil

In blender or food processor, combine first 5 ingredients; blend until onion is minced, then add oil gradually, blending until incorporated.

KAHLÚA CHEESECAKE

4 ounces butter, melted	¼ cup cocoa
2 cups graham	6 extra large eggs
cracker crumbs	¼ cup Kahlúa
3 pounds cream cheese	Whipped cream
3 cups sugar	and chocolate shavings

Line bottom of 10" cheesecake pan with parchment. Combine butter and crumbs and pat into pan; bake at 350 degrees 10 minutes. Remove and set aside. In large bowl of mixer, beat cheese until soft. Sift sugar and cocoa together; beat into cheese, scraping bowl often, until no lumps remain. Stir in eggs and Kahlúa; pour batter into pan and place in larger pan with 1" water. Bake at 350 degrees 3 hours; refrigerate overnight. To remove from pan, dip in larger pan of hot water 15 seconds; invert onto large dish and rap gently. Invert onto serving dish. Garnish each serving with ½ cup whipped cream and shavings. Serves 10.

1848 HOUSE
Marietta

Uring the hot summer of 1864, fierce battles raged from Chattanooga southward, as badly outnumbered Confederate forces retreated toward Atlanta, pursued by relentless Union General W. T. Sherman.

Although Atlanta was new, created by the junction of three railroads, it had grown rapidly, and by 1857 was known as "The Gate City".

Both sides realized the importance of the city's transportation lines, and Sherman's six-weeks' advance left little in its wake.

One of the few antebellum structures to escape destruction is a plantation house built about 1848 by John Heyward Glover, the first mayor of Marietta. During the Atlanta campaign, "Bushy Park" was occupied by William King, a son of Roswell's founder, whose prior acquaintance with Sherman is credited with its survival.

An extraordinary example of Greek Revival style, the house has a pedimented four-column Doric portico overlooking thirteen acres remaining from the original three thousand. Enlarged and remodeled in 1939, it was placed on the National Register in 1977, and was restored in 1979 to become The Planters Restaurant. It became 1848 House in 1992.

Inside, its wide staircase hall, high ceilings, and antiques— some original to the house— recall the graciousness of the Old South. Two glass-enclosed porches offer a view of the manicured grounds, if you can tear your eyes from the beautifully presented food.

Order à la carte or a four-course meal from a Contemporary Southern menu that reflects the seasons. You'll usually find rack of lamb, Filet Mignon, and pan fried quail; slow-cooked Peppered Duck is popular, as are Basil/Red Pepper Linguine with Crawfish and Tasso, and in-house Pecan-Smoked Rainbow Trout. Whatever you choose will be a carefully selected combination, individually prepared.

Clever appetizers (Georgia Shrimp with Peach Chutney, Vidalia Onion Tart), soups (Vichyssoise, Charleston "She" Crab), and salads (Caesar Salad with Cajun Fried Oysters), are just as creative, and hot homemade Sweet Potato rolls are the perfect accompaniment.

Among homemade desserts are Deep-Dish Sweet Potato Pecan Pie, Chocolate Mousse Cake, and everyone's favorite: Warm Apple Tart, topped with Cinnamon Ice Cream.

The 1848 House, 780 S. Cobb Drive (GA 280), is not visible from the road; 4.3 miles west from I-75 exit 111 (Lockheed-Dobbins) go under double overpass, take immediate right onto Pearl; gate is 300 feet on left. It is open from 6 p.m., Monday through Saturday. (404)427-4646; 428-1848. All legal beverages are available, most men wear coat and tie, and reservations are requested. AE,CB,DC,DS,MC,V. ($$$)

GRILLED SHRIMP ON YELLOW PEPPER BEURRE BLANC and GRILLED SCALLOPS ON RED PEPPER BEURRE BLANC

Black squid/burgundy
linguine, cooked al dente
12 largest sea scallops, cleaned
12 largest white shrimp,
  peeled and deveined
6 sweet yellow peppers,
  steamed
6 sweet red peppers, steamed

4 ounces unsalted butter
½ cup dry white wine
Salt and pepper
Olive oil
6 or 8 sautéed snow peas,
  diced red and yellow
  peppers, and chopped chives
  for garnish

Place scallops on 2 skewers and shrimp on 2 skewers; refrigerate covered. Skin and seed peppers, then purée separately. In small pan, place ¼ cup white wine, 2 ounces butter, and 1 ounce water. Reduce by half, add red pepper purée, salt and pepper. In another small pan, repeat, using yellow pepper purée. Lightly salt and pepper shrimp and scallops. Toss with olive oil and grill 4 to 5 minutes each side, or until just cooked. To serve, cover ½ large warm platter with red purée, other ½ with yellow purée; place linguine in center, garnished with peas and chopped peppers; place shrimp on yellow purée, and scallops on red, garnished with chives and diced peppers. Serves 4.

SMOKED SALMON CHEESECAKE

12 ounces cream cheese,
  softened
½ pound smoked salmon
  or Lox
3 eggs
½ shallot, minced
1 ounce heavy cream
1½ teaspoons lemon juice

Pinch salt
Pinch white pepper
⅛ cup sugar
Yogurt, Scallion, and
  Chive sauce*
Diced red and yellow
  peppers, green
  peppercorns, and fresh
  herbs for garnish

In mixer bowl, whip cheese until very soft. In food processor, purée salmon to paste; add eggs, 1 at a time, and shallot. Fold salmon with next 5 ingredients into cheese and blend. Pour into buttered 8" springform pan and bake in waterbath at 350 degrees 20 minutes. Remove from water; cool to room temperature, then chill at least 2 hours. To serve, cut into 6 wedges; divide sauce* among 6 plates, place wedge on each, and garnish. Serves 6.

*Sauce: in bowl, blend ½ cup plain yogurt, ¼ cup sour cream, 1 Tablespoon lemon juice, pinch each salt and white pepper, ¼ cup minced chives, ⅛ cup minceed green scallion. Chill 2 hours.

OLD VININGS INN
Vinings (Northwest Atlanta)

Hardy Pace operated a ferry across the Chattahoochee River on Cherokee land in the 1820s, long before the final Indian cession, and years before anyone dreamed of the railroad or Atlanta.

The road between his ferry and Decatur, passing through Buck Head, was an important connection; Pace built a gristmill and accumulated land, including the right-of-way for the Western and Atlantic Railroad.

On the west side of the Chattahoochee, where the tracks crossed Pace's Ferry Road, a delivery point was named "Vinings" for the railroad contractor. Nearby, Pace built a comfortable home about 1839. This house quartered Federal troops during surveillance of Atlanta, and was later a Union hospital.

From Vinings, on July 14, 1864, Union General W.T. Sherman sent out his "Special Field Orders No. 35," outlining his plan of attack. Three days later, two corps of the Army of the Cumberland crossed the Chattahoochee on a pontoon bridge at Pace's Ferry.

Pace's home was rebuilt after the War, and much of his land remains in his family. By the turn of the century, Vinings was a charming village; the railroad built a pavilion for parties and dances, and sponsored excursions.

Outings to Vinings are still popular. The Old Pavilion and several other buildings are antiques shops, and one rambling old house is the Old Vinings Inn.

In a garden-like atmosphere of chintz and pastels, bright and cheerful at lunch and romantic and candlelit in the evening, delicious food is attractively served.

You might begin with a spicy seafood chowder, or grilled eggplant with crab, and choose an entrée of chicken with artichokes; tenderloin with mushrooms, pearl onions, and Marsala; or salmon in lime butter.

Salads and sandwiches are popular at lunch, with different hot entrées daily, and desserts, which change frequently, are always special. Fresh tarts feature seasonal fruits—strawberries, blueberries, raspberries—on a cream cheese filling in a graham cracker/pecan crust; Italian cream cake is rich, with walnuts, and, for the true diehard, Chocolate Raspberry Bash: a fudgy confection, layered with raspberries and topped with chocolate sauce.

The Old Vinings Inn, 3020 Paces Mill Road, is at the corner of Paces Ferry. Lunch is 11:30 a.m. to 2:30 p.m., Monday through Saturday, dinner is 6 to 10 p.m. Monday through Thursday, until 10:30 p.m. Friday and Saturday. (404)434-5270. All legal beverages are available; Old Vinings Inn Bar across the street is also open Sundays. Reservations are recommended on weekends, and for parties of 6 or more. Busiest time is Vinings Fall Festival, first Saturday in October, and during December. AE,MC,D. ($$)

OYSTER STEW

1 pint oysters, shucked and
   drained (reserve liquor)
1 Tablespoon butter
1 Tablespoon diced shallot
¾ cup diced carrot
1½ teaspoons fresh thyme

1 quart heavy cream
4 drops Tabasco
6 drops Worcestershire
Salt and pepper
Parsley and cold butter
   for garnish

In large pot over medium heat, melt butter; add shallot and sauté 2 minutes; add carrot and sauté 2 minutes. Add cream with thyme and bring to boil; add seasonings and oyster liquor and simmer 3 or 4 minutes, or until carrots are tender. Add oysters, lower heat, and cook 2 or 3 minutes; do not overcook oysters. Taste for seasoning. Serve garnished with parsley and butter. Serves 6.

TUNA IN BLACK BEAN SALSA

1 pound dried black beans,
  prepared ahead
Salt and pepper
¼ cup diced sweet
  red pepper
¼ cup diced sweet
  yellow pepper
¼ cup diced sweet
  green pepper

¼ cup diced purple onion
¼ cup chopped cilantro
¼ cup fresh lemon juice
¼ cup fresh lime juice
4 whole jalapeño peppers,
  diced
Fresh tuna steaks or filets,
  grilled
Lime or lemon slices for
  garnish

In large, non-reactive container, mix cooked beans with remaining ingredients and refrigerate at least 4 hours. To serve, place salsa on plate, top with grilled tuna, and garnish with lime or lemon.

GROUPER ELIZABETH

Four 8-ounce grouper filets
Seasoned flour
3 ounces
  CLARIFIED margarine
4 ounces Madeira

12 ounces heavy cream
Salt and pepper
½ cup diced scallion
½ pound jumbo lump
  crab meat

Dredge grouper in flour. In large skillet over medium heat, melt margarine; when hot, place filets flesh-side down and sauté 4 minutes or until golden brown. Turn fish and cook another 2 or 3 minutes. Hold fish in warm oven until ready to serve. In another pan, flame and reduce wine by ½; add cream and reduce by ½; season; add onion and crab and cook until crab is hot. Serve over filets. Serves 4.

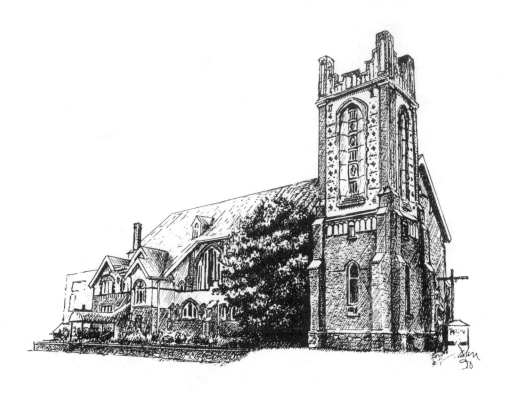

THE ABBEY
Atlanta

Confederate States President Jefferson Davis, an opinionated, vain man, had no love for anyone who differed with him. Among these was General Joseph E. Johnston, one of the Confederacy's most revered commanders.

Badly outnumbered, believing political unrest in the North would eventually aid the Confederate cause, Johnston's strategy was to hinder the enemy, gradually withdrawing, rather than attacking.

On July 17, swayed by backbiting reports and his own dislike, Davis replaced Johnston with General John Bell Hood, an able enough soldier, but totally unsuited for the job at hand.

From mid-July to mid-August, 1864, Atlanta lay under siege, bombarded by Sherman's artillery. Confederate forces left the city September 1, burning munitions trains behind them; the Union army evacuated civilians, then set fire to the remaining buildings November 14.

Atlanta was destroyed, but like its symbol, The Phoenix, rose from the ashes immediately. Within three years, it was capital of Georgia, railroads were back in operation, and its population had returned and increased. Constantly changing, never finished, Atlanta remains a testament to the vitality of the New South.

By 1918, The Ponce de Leon Avenue Methodist church, a massive dark-brick structure, occupied the southwest corner of Piedmont and Ponce de Leon avenues. It featured a rectangular tower, gothic windows and arches, and impressive stained-glass windows. Vacated in 1944, it remained empty several years, and later housed congregations from other denominations.

In 1977, Bill Swearingen relocated his well-established restaurant, The Abbey, in the former church, enhancing the ecclesiastical atmosphere with tapestry, artwork, and waiters in monk's garb. Tall brass candlesticks and a harpist in the balcony add to the effect, but the fare is far from monastic.

The Abbey's long-time staff of 100 produces exceptional contemporary Continental and Regional American food. Everything—ice creams, pastries, pastas—is made on the premises, meats are hand-cut daily, and guests may observe the kitchen staff at work through a large window.

Traditional items—fresh seafood, veal and lamb, and steaks—are still on the menu, but sauces are updated and flavorful, and presentation is breathtaking. Typical of The Abbey's flair are

Vidalia Onion soup, with sweetbread croutons; Caesar Salad featuring crisp red romaine; Grilled Gulf Coast Swordfish, sauced with oyster mushrooms, sweet peppers, Rome tomatoes and sage, then atomized with 50-year-old balsamic vinegar at tableside.

Desserts are equally inventive. A rich custard pie is layered with fresh mango, chocolate, and macadamia nuts; Frozen Banana Walnut Nougat Soufflé is topped with caramel, glazed bananas, and spikes of Lindt chocolate; and carrot cake is rich with chocolate, and frosted with chocolate cream cheese.

The Abbey, 163 Ponce de Leon, is most easily reached by the North Avenue exit from I-75; 5 blocks east, turn left at Piedmont; valet parking is on the left. It is open for dinner 7 nights a week, 6 to 10 p.m. (404)876-8532. All legal beverages are available, dress is "casual to tuxedo," and reservations are accepted but not mandatory. AE,CB,DC,DS,MC,V. ($$$)

ESCARGOT WITH SMOKED GARLIC CREAM

8 ounces unsalted butter	20 snails
4 ounces olive oil	Kosher salt
4 ounces sweet onion, in julienne	White pepper
	20 wonton wrappers
2 ounces shallot, chopped	Smoked Garlic Cream (below)
4 ounces pressed garlic	Red Pepper Coulis (below)

In saucepan, sauté first 4 ingredients until onions are translucent; add garlic until golden brown, then snails and seasonings. Bring to simmer, remove and cool completely. Wrap each cooled snail with some sauce in wonton wrapper; seal with water. In deep fryer at 350 degrees, fry until golden brown. Drain on rack. To serve, ladle Garlic Cream on 4 hot plates, surround with Red Pepper Coulis, and place 5 wonton-wrapped snails on each. At The Abbey, plate is centered with fried ginger slices and sprinkled with black sesame seeds.

SMOKED GARLIC CREAM

2 ounces garlic cloves
6 ounces unsalted butter
3 ounces sweet onion,
   in julienne
1 ounce shallot, chopped

6 ounces white wine
6 cups heavy cream
Butter
Kosher salt
White pepper

In smoker, smoke garlic over wood chips 30 minutes. Remove and cool. In skillet, sauté smoked garlic with next 3 ingredients until colorless. Deglaze with wine. Add cream, 8 ounces at a time, and reduce by ⅓. Purée in blender, strain, add a little butter and season. Yields about 4 cups.

RED PEPPER COULIS

6 ounces seeded sweet
   red pepper
2 ounces shallots

8 ounces white wine
2 ounces balsamic vinegar
Salt and pepper

In saucepan, steam first 3 ingredients; remove peppers and shallots when soft, and purée. Add vinegar and season.

THE MANSION
Atlanta

T he resurgence of Atlanta after the War Between the States was phenomenal. Ignoring the magnitude of the task and trading on the importance that had come with the War, Atlantans and those who flocked to join them replaced burned buildings and built finer ones.

The new city was flamboyant, expressive, and, above all, commercial. Enterprise and industry replaced antebellum ideals, and Atlanta's new buildings reflected this spirit, as well as the informal, picturesque architectural styles popular in other parts of the world.

Richard C. Peters, a civil engineer from Pennsylvania, had come to Georgia in 1835 to work with the Georgia Railroad. His wise purchases of railroad stock and real estate assured his family's prosperity; during the siege of Atlanta, the family was well supplied, and his wife owned "the only carriage in town," from which she distributed food to the sick and wounded.

The family's fortunes were maintained during the War, and several members continued to be prominent in charity work. A son, Edward C. Peters, inherited some of his father's vast holdings, and in 1885, built an outstanding brick High Victorian Queen Anne house on three-and-a-half acres at Piedmont and Ponce de Leon.

Possibly one of the state's finest examples of the period, the house's exterior is enriched by gables, porches, balconies, and an arched entrance influenced by Richardsonian principles. The interior, with angled rooms, embossed leather paneling, and elaborate woodwork, has a richness of design seldom seen.

The house remained in the family until 1970, and was placed on the National Register in 1972. A year later, The Mansion restaurant opened. Great care was taken to retain the charm and comfort of the original house; an octagonal pavilion, connected by a new entrance and hall, conforms to its style.

You'll fine true Southern hospitality at The Mansion, and the finest, freshest ingredients, carefully prepared and presented. Crab cakes in Beurre Blanc are topped with colorful peppers and fanned snow peas; yellow corn chowder is rich with cream and flecks of vegetables; a wide variety of crisp greens mingle in salads, and entrées are outstanding combinations.

Salmon is popular, sauced with roasted pecans or topped with scallops, or you might prefer roasted pork tenderloin with fresh apples, or Filet Mignon with chanterelles.

Among spectacular desserts is a deep, dark chocolate cake, layered with chocolate mousse and topped with white chocolate, all in a pool of raspberry coulis; and a praline basket laden with fresh fruits, ice cream, and Crème Anglaise, and named for Scarlett O'Hara.

You may never be hungry again. Think about that tomorrow.

The Mansion, 179 Ponce de Leon, is most easily reached by the North Avenue exit from I-75; 5 blocks east, its free parking lot is just past Piedmont on the left. It is open for lunch Monday through Saturday, 11 a.m. to 2 p.m.; 4-course Sunday brunch is 11 a.m. to 2:30 p.m. Dinner, 7 days a week, begins at 6 p.m.; last reservation is taken about 10:45. (404)876-0727. All legal beverages are available, dress is "cosmopolitan," and reservations are suggested. AE,DC,DS,EnRoute,JCB,MC,V. ($$$)

FRESH BERRIES
AND CHEESECAKE IN PHYLLO

Phyllo pastry
Melted butter
1 pound cream cheese
⅔ cup sugar
4 teaspoons arrowroot
1 large egg, beaten with
  1 egg yolk

2 Tablespoons vanilla
2⅓ ounces heavy cream
Raspberry sauce*
Crème Anglaise (below)
Fresh berries
8 mint sprigs

Butter eight 4-ounce baking dishes: line each with pastry sheet, brushed with butter. Extend wavy edges above dishes. In bowl of mixer, blend next 3 ingredients; mix remaining ingredients together and add to cheese mixture VERY SLOWLY. Divide into prepared cups, taking care not to break or fold pastry, and bake at 300 degrees until pastry is golden brown and cheesecake is almost firm. Cool completely before handling. To serve, spread raspberry sauce* on 8 dessert plates; carefully remove dishes and place pastry-wrapped cheesecakes on plates. Drop fresh berries (strawberries, blueberries, raspberries & blackberries) on top. Using squeeze bottle, squirt Crème Anglaise over everything. Garnish with mint.

*For a similar raspberry sauce, see J. Henry's Restaurant.

CRÈME ANGLAISE

2 cups heavy cream   ½ cup sugar, divided
½ vanilla bean, split   4 eggs

In top of double boiler over medium heat, place cream; scrape seeds from vanilla bean and add seeds and bean to cream with ¼ cup sugar. Mix eggs with remaining sugar; warm with some of the heated cream, then return all to pot and cook, stirring constantly, until thickened. DO NOT BOIL. Strain and chill. Yields about 3 cups; may be served with many desserts or alone.

THE MAGNOLIA TEA ROOM
Stone Mountain Village

Georgia's most noticeable natural landmark, a single piece of granite two miles long and more than 800 feet high, looms above the treetops, visible for miles; it is the largest piece of exposed granite in the world.

Long a meeting place for Creek Indians, by 1790 it had attracted European settlers, who called it "Rock Mountain." It was renamed Stone Mountain in 1825, when it was a tourist attraction and the village at its base was a resort for visitors who arrived by regular stagecoach.

The village relocated to trackside when the Georgia Rail Road came through in 1845; granite quarried from mountain ledges could then be shipped readily, and tourism lost its importance. Interrupted by the War, the quarrying business changed hands several times afterward, but grew to a huge industry, with stonecutters imported from Europe, and its own railway to transport them and the stone.

Stone Mountain granite was used in the rebuilding of Atlanta, locks of the Panama Canal, the east wing of the U.S. Capitol, and in numerous other buildings all over the world, as well as the village's own depot, now the City Hall.

A simple one-story, four-room frame cottage with an inset porch was built on the road from the village to the mountain, reportedly about 1854, by George Smith, bookkeeper and accountant for the granite company. The charming little dwelling, set back from the street in a grove of trees, shows elements of Greek Revival in its structure, but its proportions and trim are Victorian.

After the death of its last residential owner, the house was threatened with demolition, but was rescued by Nancy Myers and her daughter, Debbie, who renovated it and opened Magnolia Tea Room in 1989. It was expanded by a large rear addition in 1990 to accommodate weddings and private parties, as well as the bountiful Sunday Brunch Buffet.

With the staff enlarged by Chef Biff Permenter (now married to Debbie), the tea room presents New American-Continental food that is fresh, inventive and plentiful. Robust entrées—Snapper Szechuan, grilled ribeye steak with burgundy mushrooms and onions, Chicken Pot Pie in puff pastry—are accompanied by vegetable, starch, and wonderful homemade breads.

Soups are rich and savory, changing frequently, Smoked

Salmon Pasta Salad is tangy with horseradish and dill, and Spinach Salad has a sautéed chicken liver-bacon dressing.

The Magnolia Salad Plate, perhaps the most popular lunch item, contains tasty chicken salad in a heart-shaped puff pastry, with frozen fruit salad, new potato salad, fresh fruit and spiced bread.

Most desserts are made by Nancy; you never know what you'll find, but recurring favorites include fresh fruit cobbler, Chocolate Syrup Cake, Hazelnut Grand Marnier Torte, and Banana Cheesecake, topped with Praline Sauce.

Magnolia Tea Room, 5459 E. Mountain Street, is less than 1 mile from the West Gate of Stone Mountain Park, 3 blocks from Main Street. It is open for lunch Tuesday through Saturday, 11 a.m. to 2:30 p.m., for dinner Friday, 5:30 to 9 p.m., and for Sunday brunch 11 a.m. to 2:30 p.m. (404)498-6304. Dress is "nice casual," wine, champagne, and beer are available, and reservations are appreciated for groups greater than 4. It is closed a week in early September, and for the week between Christmas and New Years'. No credit cards accepted; personal checks accepted. ($$)

TOMATO BASIL BISQUE

1 large yellow onion, chopped
1 Tablespoon chopped basil
1 teaspoon pepper
3 Tablespoons olive oil
28-ounce can whole tomatoes,
  chopped

28-ounce can tomato purée
4 cups chicken stock
½ cup roux*
2 cups heavy cream

In stock pot, sauté first 3 ingredients in oil. Add next 3 ingredients, bring to a boil, reduce heat and simmer 20 minutes. Increase heat to high and whisk in roux. Boil 5 minutes, stirring often. Reduce heat, add cream, taste for salt, and serve. Serves 12 to 14.

*Roux: mix 4 ounces melted butter with ¾ cup flour.

SUNDAY BRUNCH SAUSAGE, EGG, AND CHEESE CASSEROLE

1 pound Jimmy Dean™ sausage	2 teaspoons salt
1 dozen eggs	1 teaspoon pepper
2 cups milk	12 slices whole wheat bread
	2 cups shredded cheddar cheese

In skillet, cook sausage, chopping with a spoon to crumble. Drain fat and set aside. Whisk eggs, milk, and seasonings. Line casserole dish with 4 slices bread, sprinkle with sausage and cheese, and repeat, using all. Pour in egg mixture and bake at 350 degrees 45 minutes to one hour. Cut into squares. Serves 12.

THE FREIGHT ROOM
Decatur

W hen the Georgia Rail Road extended its line westward in 1845, the tracks passed south of Decatur, giving rise to the erroneous belief that had citizens been less concerned about the noise and dirt of railroads, Decatur would have become the metropolis, rather than Atlanta.

The original "terminus" of the Western and Atlantic Railroad, however, was designated "at some point not exceeding eight miles from the southeast bank of the Chattahoochee," and its junction with two other lines was what created the "Gate City of the South."

By 1850, Atlanta had a population of 6,000, and having to travel to Decatur (population 750) to handle legal matters was burdensome. Fulton County was formed from Dekalb in 1853, with Atlanta as its seat.

Decatur developed its own identity as a "healthful, beautiful, and agreeable village," and as a center of culture and learning.

The Decatur Female Seminary opened in 1889, and the following year, Colonel George Washington Scott made a substantial donation to the school. Agnes Scott Hall, named for his mother, was completed in 1891; the school's name was changed to honor her. In 1906, it became a four-year college, and its academic program and graduates have given it an outstanding reputation.

The same year the school opened also marked construction of the new Georgia Railroad depot, diagonally across the tracks. Built on the site of an earlier station burned during the War, the one-story frame building, of typical railroad design, housed offices, waiting rooms, and a freight room, where baggage was weighed, labeled, and loaded.

It was in that end of the building that Wade Wright opened his restaurant in 1981; four years later, when the railroad moved its offices, the entire building became The Freight Room.

Its board-and-batten siding painted a pleasant green, trimmed with cream, the little station now sports a deck on its eastern end. Outdoors and indoors, The Freight Room is a popular gathering spot; frequent music performances are a draw, but most folks come for the good food and friendly atmosphere.

Surrounded by railroad memorabilia (even a functioning "N" gauge layout on the bar) visitors enjoy two dozen savory, unusual soups (Salmon Chowder!) that rotate on the menu.

Choose-your-own-everything deli sandwiches are popular,

as are generous "Melts" of tuna, vegetable, or chicken and avocado, but there are plenty of choices. You might try delicious Christie's Chicken Salad, incorporating grapes and apples, or Vegetable Lasagna, or the evening's entrée special that reflects the night's music: Cajun music and Gumbo, for instance.

Finish up with a piece of spicy homemade apple pie with vanilla bean ice cream, settle back, and enjoy yourself. The Freight Room is the right place for it.

The Freight Room, 301 E. Howard Avenue, is at the corner of East College Avenue and S. Candler Road It is open 7 days a week, with continuous service: 11 a.m. to 11 p.m. Monday through Friday, 12 N to 1 a.m. Saturday, and 12 N to 12 M Sunday. (404)378-5365. Dress is casual, all legal beverages are available, and reservations are not accepted. There is entertainment Wednesday through Sunday; Thursday is bluegrass music night. AE,MC,V. ($)

TURKEY AND RICE SOUP

8 cups turkey or chicken stock   ½ cup raw rice
4 cups cooked turkey, cubed   1 teaspoon parsley
3 medium carrots, chopped   ¼ teaspoon garlic salt
1 stalk celery, chopped   ¼ teaspoon onion salt
½ cup chopped scallions   ¼ teaspoon pepper
  ½ bay leaf

In stockpot, bring first 5 ingredients to boil, lower heat, and simmer 30 minutes. Add rice and remaining ingredients and simmer about 1 hour or until vegetables are tender. Serves 8 to 10.

SHRIMP GALUCKI

1 pound cooked rotini pasta
1 pound cooked,
  peeled shrimp
1½ cups chopped celery
1 cup minced scallions
1 medium green pepper,
  minced

2 hard-cooked eggs, grated
5 Tablespoons mayonnaise
2 Tablespoons tarragon
1 Tablespoon garlic salt
1½ teaspoons onion salt
1½ teaspoons pepper

In large bowl, mix first 6 ingredients. In small bowl, whisk remaining ingredients. Add dressing to pasta mixture until just blended. Refrigerate at least 2 hours. Stir well before serving.

PACIFIC COAST LINE SANDWICH

4 ripe avocados,
  peeled and pitted
1 Tablespoon lemon juice
2 Tablespoons sour cream
¾ teaspoon pepper
¾ teaspoon garlic salt

¾ teaspoon onion salt
Fresh rye bread
Alfalfa sprouts
Sliced tomatoes
Sliced Monterey jack
  cheese, optional

In bowl, mash avocado with lemon juice; leave chunky. Add next 4 ingredients and refrigerate. To assemble, spread avocado mixture on bread, top with sprouts, tomato slices, optional cheese, and second slice of bread.

FINNIGAN'S JUNCTION
Covington

As the western frontiers of Georgia expanded, transportation of produce from new farming regions became a problem—some of the richest land was isolated from navigable water.

Simultaneously, interest in railroads was growing throughout the world. The country's first steam-powered train, the "Best Friend of Charleston," made its initial run in 1830; Georgia needed railroads to compete.

The Georgia Rail Road and Banking Company was chartered in 1833 to connect Athens with Augusta, where freight could be ferried across the Savannah River to the South Carolina Railroad, or shipped downriver to Savannah.

In 1836, the Western and Atlantic Railroad was chartered to operate between the Tennessee River at Chattanooga and the Chattahoochee River, and the Georgia Rail Road extended its line to connect with it. This "Terminus," later named "Marthasville," eventually became the city of Atlanta.

The route of the Georgia Rail Road, hotly debated, finally ran between Covington and Oxford, where Emory College was located. The college sold the railroad several hundred acres, and by 1849, it was the second busiest freight station, third busiest passenger station on the main line.

A new station, built about 1855, was damaged during the War Between the States; it was repaired and functioning by 1868. A portion of the station destroyed by fire in 1884 was replaced by a brick structure, still in use when passenger service ended in 1983.

Sold in 1985, the depot housed several short-lived restaurants before brothers Mike and Jeff Crowe bought and extensively reconditioned the dilapidated building in 1988. With an open interior divided into cozy seating areas, the old depot belies its size; dark brown ceilings, exposed brick walls, and lots of natural wood create a friendly, comfortable atmosphere.

You can be yourself at Finnigan's Junction. If you want soup and salad and the rest of your party wants steaks or ribs, or if you have dietary restrictions, or a small child, they can handle it.

The sixty-five item menu changes every three months, but the quality and the service are always consistent. "We buy the best products available," Mike says, "and prepare everything as fresh as possible."

Homemade soups—French Onion, a superb Black Bean,

Cauliflower/Cheese, and Seafood Bisque, to name a few—are piping hot, as is Chili Pot Pie, in a toasted bread bowl. Combine with a half-sandwich for a quick lunch (most lunches prepared in less than 15 minutes) or choose from pasta, southwestern, or seafood entrées.

House specialty prime rib, slow-baked with garlic and pepper, is claimed to be "the best in Atlanta." Steaks are hand-cut, and fish, delivered fresh daily, will be prepared any way you want it.

Most entrées come "with" extras, but try to save room for dessert. There are at least six every day; you might find White Chocolate Pecan Pie, delectable Lemon Mousse Pie, or a Chocolate Turtle Cake simply gooey with caramel and nuts.

Finnigan's Junction, 4122 N. Emory Street, is open 11 a.m. to 10:30 p.m., Monday through Thursday, to 11:30 Friday and Saturday, with continuous service. (404)784-1128. Dress is casual, all legal beverages are available, and there is a preferred seating policy, with waits of no more than 25 minutes. Reservations accepted only for parties of 8 or more. There is entertainment in the bar 5 nights a week. AE,DS,MC,V. ($)

FRIED CHILI PEPPERS

6 or 8 large banana or chili peppers	Oil
	2 cups flour
8 to 12 ounces Monterey jack cheese, cubed	10 ounce box tempura batter mix, prepared
2 cups milk	Bottled salsa

Slice peppers 2 inches in center; hollow out all seeds, not breaking pepper. Stuff with cheese and soak in milk. In skillet, heat 1" oil over medium heat; roll peppers in flour, dip in batter to coat, and fry in oil until golden brown on both sides. Serve with salsa. Serves 4.

KAT'S CHICKEN SALAD

Four 8-ounce chicken
   breasts, baked and diced
1 medium onion, diced
2 celery stalks, diced
2 scallions, chopped
2 cups mayonnaise

¾ cup sour cream
1 teaspoon garlic salt
½ teaspoon celery salt
½ teaspoon onion salt
2 pinches white pepper
¼ cup chopped walnuts

In large bowl, combine all ingredients and chill 1 hour. If too thick, thin with a little mayonnaise. Serves 4 to 6.

SKILLET-BLACKENED SCALLOPS

8 to 10 ounces
   medium scallops
¼ cup olive oil
2 scallions, chopped

1 stalk broccoli, sliced thin
Blackening spice
Tabasco and red pepper
   flakes, optional

In skillet, sauté scallops in oil until firm. Add vegetables, and sprinkle on blackening spice to desired strength. For extra heat, add Tabasco and red pepper to taste. Serve with rice.
Serves 2 or 3.

BILLIE'S BLUE WILLOW INN
Social Circle

The intersection of Etowah Hightower Trail and Rogue Road was important to Native Americans until 1818, when they renounced their claims to the land. In December of that year, Walton County was created, and land was distributed by a lottery.

Lot 96, containing the crossroads and a spring, grew into the village of Social Circle. Incorporated in 1832, it had a burst of growth when the Georgia Rail Road came through in 1845.

During the Atlanta Campaign, railroad access to the city had been halted; leaving the city in flames, Federals on their "March to the Sea," continued the destruction. On November 18, 1864, Sherman's Left Wing reached Social Circle, the nearest functional point on the Georgia Rail Road; they burned the depot, and destroyed the tracks east to Madison.

Rebuilding was quick after the War, and Social Circle had a second boom, during which ante-bellum frame commercial structures were replaced by brick ones, and many of the town's fine homes were constructed.

John Upshaw built a handsome two-story Neoclassical house of yellow brick on the east side of North Cherokee around the turn of the century. Fluted Corinthian columns on its two-story portico, leaded-glass fanlights and sidelights, and generously proportioned rooms made it a showplace. As part of the Social Circle Historic District, it was placed on the National Register in 1980.

The house had been a community center and a church when Billie and Louis Van Dyke bought it; Billie's Blue Willow Inn opened on Thanksgiving Day, 1991, and has been serving mouth-watering traditional Southern buffets to hungry folks ever since.

The sideboard and huge tables groan with silver and crystal bowls of salads and memorable vegetables—REAL hand-mashed potatoes, candied yams, fried green tomatoes, fresh greens, Lima beans, Harvard beets and "whatever's in season"—and entrées such as Orange Pecan Chicken on wild rice, baked whole salmon, roast pork, Seafood au Gratin, Savannah Shrimp and Rice, and, always, fried chicken.

A meal at Billie's is like visiting a favorite aunt in childhood; there's everything you remember, even side dishes of homemade fig preserves and tomato chutney. And not since childhood have you experienced such desserts: peach cobbler, Billie's Hot Brownie Pie, Southern banana pudding, pineapple upside-down cake. . . .

Take your Yankee friends. THIS is The South.

101

Billie's Blue Willow Inn, 294 N. Cherokee Road (GA 11), is open for lunch 11 a.m. to 2 p.m., Monday through Saturday, 11 a.m. to 3 p.m. Sunday. Dinner, Thursday through Saturday, is 5:30 to 9 p.m. Hours may be longer in summer. (404)464-2131. Dress is casual to dressy, and reservations are requested for parties of 15 or more. No credit cards accepted; personal checks accepted. ($)

SKILLET SQUASH

1 to 1½ yellow squash per person	1 small onion, thinly sliced
¾ cup melted butter, divided	4 slices bacon, fried crisp & chopped
1 ounce bacon grease	Salt and pepper

Wash and slice squash, discarding ends. In large skillet, cook 1 cup water, ½ cup butter, bacon grease, and onion until onion is tender. Add squash, bacon, and seasonings. Cook until desired tenderness. Drain. Pour remaining butter over squash and serve.

COLLARD GREENS

Large bunch collards	½ teaspoon salt
8 ounces "fat back" pork	1 Tablespoon sugar
1 ounce bacon grease	¼ teaspoon pepper
	¼ teaspoon baking powder

Remove stems from collard leaves and discard. Wash thoroughly in cold water and tear into small pieces. Place in large pot with 1 quart water and remaining ingredients. Cook until tender, stirring occasionally. Serves 6 to 8.

MACARONI AND CHEESE

8-ounce package macaroni
1 Tablespoon
   vegetable shortening
1 pound grated
   mild cheddar, divided

¾ cup milk
4 eggs, beaten
1 teaspoon salt
¼ teaspoon white pepper
1 Tablespoon mayonnaise
½ teaspoon mustard

Cook macaroni according to package directions, adding shortening to water. Do not overcook. Drain, and mix with previously combined remaining ingredients, saving enough cheese for topping. Bake uncovered, in ungreased casserole, at 350 degrees 35 to 40 minutes, or until firm. Top with reserved cheese and return to oven to melt. Serves 6 to 8.

PEACH COBBLER

1½ cups self-rising flour
About 1½ cups sugar,
   divided

About 1½ cups butter,
   divided
29-ounce can
   sliced peaches, with juice

In bowl, blend flour and 1 cup sugar; work in melted butter until mixture is yellow and crumbly but not gummy. Sprinkle ⅓ of this mixture on bottom of ungreased casserole; add peaches and about ¼ cup butter. Sprinkle ½ cup sugar on top and cover with remaining flour mixture. Sprinkle with remaining butter and a little sugar and bake, uncovered, at 350 degrees about 30 minutes, or until golden. Serves 6 to 8.

THE YESTERDAY CAFÉ
Rutledge

The Rutledge family came to Georgia from South Carolina, the first of several families from that area to settle in Morgan County. When the Georgia Rail Road was built, the "turnaround," where trains took on fuel and water, was near Miss Polly Rutledge's log cabin.

Workers soon referred to the location as "Rutledge," a town developed around the railroad, and the Vining House hotel attracted visitors who could count on good food and friendly townspeople.

The Soloman Dewald Masonic Lodge, established in Rutledge in 1893, was named for its founder, and the building constructed for the second-floor lodge hall, a simple two-story brick structure, housed a drugstore on the first floor, with a doctor's office in the rear.

Local businessman Tommy Breedlove saw a need for a restaurant in Rutledge; the Masons offered him their vacant first floor, and the Yesterday Café was born.

Charmingly decorated by Judy Breedlove with appropriate antiques and framed pictures from Rutledge's past, it is part of the downtown rejuvenation accomplished in just seven years.

Funded by the Rutledge Country Fair, trees, brick sidewalks, curbs, and signs are in place, and interesting new shops occupy buildings unused for years. Once again, visitors enjoy friendly people and good food, often staying for golf, swimming, and camping at nearby Hard Labor Creek State Park.

Locals and visitors appreciate "Modern Country" food at the Yesterday Café, in which fresh southern ingredients appear in non-traditional combinations, all made from "scratch." Catfish filets are baked in an herb crust; chicken croquettes are served in a creamy tomato sauce over pasta; and filet mignon coated with parsley and cracked pepper is seared on a griddle. Entrées come with red potatoes braised in chicken stock and onions, seasonal vegetables, and fresh, homemade bread.

Lunchtime favorites include sandwiches and burgers, wonderful soups and salads, and specials—one is a particularly good chicken pot pie—the same sundae bar and great homemade desserts you'll find at night, and tiny sweet Peach Puffs as soon as you sit down.

Who says the "good old days" are gone?

The Yesterday Café, 120 Fairplay Road, is easily reached from exit 49 off I-20. It is open for breakfast and lunch, Monday through Friday, 7 a.m. to 2 p.m., Saturday and Sunday, 8 a.m. to 3 p.m. "Supper" is served Thursday through Saturday, 5:30 to 10:30 p.m. (706)557-9337. Dress is casual, reservations are accepted (encouraged for large groups and for supper), and busiest time is during the Rutledge Country Fair, Memorial Day Weekend. MC,V. ($)

REAL CORNED BEEF HASH
"OUR DELUXE BREAKFAST"

1 pound cooked corned beef, diced

2 pounds cooked red potatoes, skin on, diced

½ medium yellow onion, diced

Black pepper

Oil

4 eggs

In bowl, mix first 4 ingredients; place in hot non-stick pan and pour a little oil around edge. Shake pan, then cook without stirring over medium-high heat until browned. Turn hash over; make four small indentations and break an egg into each. Cover and cook until eggs are cooked. Yields 4 large portions.

CARIBBEAN CHICKEN SALAD

5-ounce bottle Pickapeppa™ sauce

1½ cups honey

16 ounces purchased vinaigrette dressing

Eight 6-ounce skinless, boneless chicken breasts

Salad mixture—mixed greens, sliced onion, tomato wedges, croutons, crumbled bacon, sliced green pepper

In screw-top quart jar, mix Pickapeppa sauce with honey; shake well. Measure 1 cup of this mixture and mix with vinaigrette; set aside. Pour remaining mixture over chicken breasts and marinate overnight in non-reactive pan. When ready to serve, divide salad mixture among 8 chilled plates. Cook chicken—pan-fry, grill, broil, or charbroil—about 4 minutes each side, slice ⅛" thin, and sprinkle one breast over each salad. Serve with reserved dressing. Serves 8.

BRAISED RED CABBAGE

Large yellow onion,
  sliced ⅛" thick
⅔ cup sugar
1 medium head red
  cabbage, cored and
  sliced ⅛" thick

Pinch powdered clove
¼ teaspoon nutmeg
1 teaspoon white pepper
⅓ cup cider vinegar

In large pan, cook onion with sugar until sugar is clear. Add remaining ingredients and cook 20 minutes over medium-low heat, stirring often. Serve as side dish. Especially good with sausage, duck, or any cured meat. Keeps 2 weeks in refrigerator.

CHOCOLATE CHIP BREAD PUDDING

4 eggs, beaten
¾ cup sugar
½ teaspoon vanilla
½ teaspoon cinnamon
¼ teaspoon nutmeg
4 cups milk, scalded

8 large day-old biscuits,
  broken
1 cup semi-sweet
  chocolate chips
1-pound jar
  dark fudge topping

Mix first 5 ingredients; stir in hot milk. In buttered 9" x 12" Pyrex dish, layer biscuits with chips. Pour in custard and let stand 20 minutes. Bake at 325 degrees 1 hour. Heat topping and spread over warm pudding. Serve warm with cream, if desired. Serves 8 to 12.

LA MAISON ON TELFAIR
Augusta

Fort Augusta, authorized by Georgia Trustees in 1736, was built near an Indian trading post 150 miles upriver from Savannah, and was named for the Princess of Wales.

Richmond County was formed from St. Paul's Parish in 1777, and Augusta was named county seat. When the 1801 courthouse was replaced, it became a private residence, and the property surrounding it was divided.

In 1854, one lot was sold to Jesse Osmond, a master builder, who evidently built the present house before he moved to Savannah in 1858. It was purchased twice for widows who lived there with their children, then was home to a mill owner. In 1884 it was sold to Louis A. Gardelle, a druggist, whose family lived in the house until the 1970s, when it first became a restaurant. As part of the "Pinched Gut" Historic District, it was placed on the National Register in 1980.

An appealing two-story frame house with a gable roof and an unusual porch, it has elements of Greek Revival style; now, decorated in peach and Venetian red, its dining rooms are timelessly romantic.

You'll fall in love with the marvelous food.

European-trained chef-owner Heinz Sowinski believes in a lot of attention to detail, and it shows. Steaks are cut to order, served with your choice of sauce, and special diets are accommodated effortlessly and creatively: Swedish Cucumber salad has no oil, tangy Raspberry Vinaigrette is an oil-free dressing, and low-fat buffalo and antelope tenderloins are sauced with a port wine-rosemary-juniper berry reduction that has neither cream nor flour, but plenty of taste.

Those who don't have to worry about diet will relish the abundance of complex, classically prepared dishes and rich European pastries and desserts.

Chocolate Velvet is filled with a rum ganache, topped with a white chocolate rose; European fruit tarts feature white chocolate amaretto mousse; and trifle-like Tira Misú is beyond description.

La Maison on Telfair, 404 Telfair Street, is open Monday through Saturday, 6 to 10:30 p.m. (706)722-4805. All legal beverages are available, dress is "casually elegant" (jacket strongly suggested for men), and reservations are preferred, especially for holidays and romantic occasions. Busiest time is The Masters golf tournament, 1st week in

April. The restaurant is closed 2 weeks in July, approx. July 4 to 20. AE,MC,V. ($$$)

OYSTERS IMPERIAL

1 Tablespoon
  chopped shallots
1 teaspoon olive oil
2 teaspoons brandy
1½ Hellmann's™
  mayonnaise
3 eggs, beaten

½ sweet red pepper, diced
3 scallions, diced
1½ cups grated Swiss cheese
2 teaspoons
  Worcestershire sauce
1 cup clean-picked
  lump blue crab meat
60 oysters, in the shell

In small skillet, brown shallot in oil; add brandy, flame, and cool. In large bowl, blend all ingredients except oysters. Open oysters and rinse in cold salty water. Place 1 heaping Tablespoon of mixture on each oyster on shell. Bake at 425 degrees 7 to 10 minutes, until golden brown. Serves 10.

Chef's note: an excellent topping for chicken breast.

RACK OF LAMB, MONGOLIAN STYLE

2 racks of lamb
1 Tablespoon
  chopped rosemary
1½ teaspoons thyme

1 Tablespoon oregano
1½ teaspoons basil
Salt and fresh-ground pepper
Apricot glaze*

Remove all fat from rack. In bowl, blend herbs; rub generously into meat and refrigerate overnight in plastic bag. Remove from bag, season, and bake at 425 degrees 15 to 20 minutes (medium rare for 2-pound rack). Baste with glaze* after 15 minutes; return to oven 5 minutes to brown. Serves 4.

Apricot Glaze: in saucepan, blend 4 ounces apricot jam, 1 teaspoon minced fresh ginger, 1 clove garlic, crushed, 2 ounces white wine, and 1 ounce soy sauce. Simmer 10 minutes. Use to baste, and serve as a sauce over carved meat.

Chef's note: lamb leg or loin may be substituted. For best results, use fresh herbs.

CRÈME BRULÉE

21 ounces heavy cream
21 ounces
  half and half cream
½ vanilla bean, split

11 egg yolks
11 ounces sugar
2 ounces triple sec liqueur
Zest of ½ orange
10 teaspoons sugar

In large, heavy pan, bring first 3 ingredients to a boil, while STIRRING (do not beat) next 4 ingredients in a large bowl with wire whip. Ladle hot cream slowly into egg mixture, stirring constantly. Allow mixture to settle until bubbles have disappeared. Ladle into 10 dishes, stirring from bottom to distribute vanilla and zest evenly. Bake in waterbath at 300 to 325 degrees about 1 hour; custard should not brown or bubble. When consistency is like heavy sour cream, remove and cool. Just before serving, sprinkle each with 1 teaspoon sugar and broil WHILE WATCHING until sugar caramelizes, just a few seconds. Serve with a few fresh raspberries or strawberries, if desired.

THE PARTRIDGE INN
Augusta

After the Revolution, Augusta, first Capital of Georgia, was a cosmopolitan town, its cultural advantages balanced by commerce and industry. Prominent Georgians, including Signer of the Declaration of Independence George Walton and Governor John Milledge, built homes in the sand hills above town.

"Summerville" benefitted from a climate thought to prevent yellow fever; it offered, at least, an escape from the "putrid effluvia" of rotting cottonseed and other summer odors. A retreat for social Southerners, it acquired electric lights, stores, and hotels when wealthy Northerners came for winters in the late 1800s.

On the side of "The Hill," lot 8 was sold to Daniel Meigs in 1816; after his death, his brother Johnathan lived there, joined by another brother, Return J. Meigs, before 1850. The property passed out of the Meigs family in 1861, and changed hands six times before 1900.

Morris Partridge, cashier of the Bon Air Hotel across the street, obtained the Meigs house about 1900, opened it as an inn in 1907, and began increasing its size in 1909. The Partridge Hotel hosted social events for generations, achieving 129 rooms and five floors by 1929. It deteriorated after World War II, and became an apartment house in the 1960s.

As part of the Summerville Historic District, the building was placed on the National Register in 1980. Threatened with demolition, it was rescued by a $6 million rehabilitation, and in 1988 again became an elegant hotel, known for outstanding food.

In the crisp white and mauve second-floor dining room, wide windows open onto verandas overlooking the city, and fresh local ingredients create an updated Southern cuisine. Hot popovers precede aged beef, fresh vegetables, and fresh seafoods, all prepared to order with thought for the diner's health.

Popular entrées include spinach fettuccine tossed with steamed veggies and basil pesto, or with sautéed shrimp, scallops, and crab meat; and medallions of beef topped with crab, scallions, and mushrooms, covered with Hollandaise.

"Southern Sweets" are temptations: Chocolate Bread Pudding, Peanut Butter Pie, and Chocolate Nut Torte with whiskey sauce and whipped cream.

The Partridge Inn, 2110 Walton Way, is open 7 days a week. Breakfast is 6:30 to 9 a.m., lunch and Sunday brunch are 11:30 a.m. to 2:30 p.m., afternoon tea, Monday through Saturday, is 3 to 5 p.m.; dinner is 6 to 10 p.m., to 11 p.m. Friday and Saturday. (706)737-8888, (800)476-6888. All legal beverages are available, most men wear coat and tie, and reservations are requested, a necessity during The Masters golf tournament, 1st week in April. There are 105 overnight suites. AE,CB,DC,MC,V. ($$)

SMOKED SALMON TARTARE

1 to 1½ pounds
  smoked salmon, chopped
Whites of 3 hard-cooked eggs
  finely chopped
3½ ounces capers,
  finely chopped
About ½ cup chopped parsley

2 chive sprigs, finely chopped
Juice of ½ lemon
1 Tablespoon
  extra virgin olive oil
1 Tablespoon
  raspberry vinegar
1 clove garlic, pressed
Pepper

In large bowl, mix all ingredients and refrigerate. Absorb or strain out excess juices before serving. Place on platter with Bremer™ Wafers. Serves 8 as appetizer.

MANGO AND TOMATO SALAD
WITH BASIL CURRY DRESSING

4 ripe plum tomatoes, cored
1 large ripe mango
1½ Tablespoons
  extra-virgin olive oil

1 teaspoon white wine vinegar
Pinch curry powder
4 to 6 large basil leaves
Salt and pepper

Cut tomatoes into ½" wedges. Cut mango from pit in ½" slices; remove skin. Alternate mango and tomato slices on plate. Using mortar and pestle, combine remaining ingredients until basil is pulverized. Drizzle dressing over mangoes and tomatoes and serve immediately. Serves 4.

CRÈME BRULÉE

2 cups half and half cream
1 quart heavy cream
5 ounces sugar

1½ Tablespoons vanilla
Yolks of 12 eggs
Sugar

In top of double boiler, WARM first 4 ingredients. Pour 1 cup of warm mixture into bowl of egg yolks; beat together, then pour into remaining warm cream. Stir and pour into 8 4-ounce soufflé cups. Bake in waterbath at 325 degrees about 20 to 25 minutes, or until custard is absolutely firm. To serve, sprinkle 1 Tablespoon sugar on each custard. Put under broiler until sugar melts; sugar should harden when removed from broiler. Serve with raspberry sauce, if desired. Serves 8.

THE WHITE ELEPHANT CAFÉ
Augusta

Even the rudimentary town of Augusta laid out by the British had a "Broad" Street 350 feet wide, intended as a parade ground. It was eventually reduced to 170 feet, but travelers were still impressed by its width, the trees on either side and in its central park, and the variety of buildings down its length.

The falls of the Savannah River provided power for industry, and navigable waters downriver made Augusta the shipping center for most of the state. It was expected to be the "metropolis" of Georgia, and Broad Street was its center of commerce.

As population increased, Broad Street grew to the west, and by late nineteenth century was populated with homes and small shops.

Development just after World War I included the center of the 1100 block of Broad. Several businesses were demolished to make way for a block of four contiguous three-story brick buildings, each with commercial space on the first floor and living space above.

The westernmost building housed a dry goods store until 1965, when it was briefly used for appliance sales, followed by twenty years as a tavern and pool room. As part of the Broad Street Historic District, the block was placed on the National Register in 1980.

The end building was purchased in 1990, and intelligent rehabilitation has returned the ground floor of the block to attractive commercial space. Renovation of upstairs apartments is underway.

The White Elephant Café, named for a long-time business formerly next door, is operated by Spencer Shadden and Amy Bliven. Believing that high quality and exciting flavor need not be expensive, they provide "Global food with an American twist" in a fresh, bistro environment.

With menu and blackboard to choose from, there's a world of variety—and a lot of surprises. The "Express Lunch," a complete meal of home cooked entrée, salad, starch, and vegetable, might be "somebody's mom's meatloaf" with REAL mashed potatoes and gravy.

Soups are savory and unexpected, sandwiches creative combinations, and desserts are like you wish mother had made: peanut butter mousse in an Oreo cookie crust, Grand Marnier torte, and homemade peach ice cream.

117

There's "something international every day," with appropriate background music on Worldly Wednesdays when an ethnic cuisine is featured. Whether you want a quick lunch or a candlelit dinner, you'll be delighted.

The White Elephant Café, 1135 Broad Street, is open for lunch, Tuesday through Friday and for Saturday brunch 11:30 a.m. to 2:30 p.m. Dinner, Friday and Saturday, is 6 to 9:30 p.m. (706)722-8614. Dress is "casual in good taste," beer and wine are available, and reservations are accepted, but not required. Busiest time is The Masters golf tournament, 1st week in April. AE,V, personal checks. ($)

WALNUT-SPINACH PESTO

8 cups loosely packed
  fresh basil leaves
8 cups loosely packed spinach
¾ cup walnuts
  (or use half pinenuts)

6 Tablespoons minced garlic
1 cup grated Parmesan cheese
¾ cup olive oil
Salt

In food processor, combine first 5 ingredients. Add olive oil slowly, in a steady stream, while processor is running, until a smooth paste is formed. Season to taste. Use to season pasta, salads, etc.

PASTA ANGELICA

Angel hair pasta,
  cooked al dente
2 Tablespoons olive oil
⅛ cup julienne red onion
⅛ cup julienne carrot
⅛ cup julienne
  sweet red pepper
¼ cup julienne zucchini
¼ cup julienne yellow squash
½ cup sliced mushrooms

6 to 8 ounces peeled,
  deveined shrimp
Dash of white wine
1 Tablespoon minced garlic
6 ounces crab meat
4 to 6 ounces smoked salmon,
  sliced thin
½ to ⅔ cup heavy cream
Dash of Parmesan cheese
1½ teaspoons pesto (above)
Salt

In 10" skillet, heat oil, add next 5 ingredients, and sauté lightly. Add next 3 ingredients, and sauté; add next 5 ingredients and simmer 3 to 5 minutes over low heat. Stir in pesto, and season to taste. Serve on pasta, tossing if desired.

APPLE CRISP

9-inch unbaked pie crust
3 to 4 large
   Granny Smith apples
Juice of ½ lemon
⅓ cup sugar
½ teaspoon cinnamon

½ cup brown sugar
¾ cup flour
1 cup oatmeal
2 pinches allspice
½ teaspoon cinnamon
Dash nutmeg
½ cup softened margarine

Peel apples and slice (¼ to ½") into large bowl. Squeeze in lemon juice; add sugar and cinnamon, toss, and set aside. In another bowl, combine brown sugar, flour, oats, and spices. Cut in butter until uniform in texture. Fill crust with apples and any juice; sprinkle with topping and pack down, completely covering apples. Bake 45 minutes to 1 hour, until crust is golden and apples are tender.

THE MAPLE STREET MANSION
Carrollton

Carroll County was formed from hotly contested Creek Indian Cessions of 1825 and '26, although legal possession did not occur until 1828. The county and its seat, Carrollton, were named for Charles Carroll, Signer of the Declaration of Independence from Maryland.

Among original settlers was a New Englander, Appleton Mandeville. In 1833, he brought maple saplings with him to plant around the new home called "Maple Hill."

His third son, Leroy Clifton Mandeville, born in 1851, became one of the area's most prominent citizens. A founder of the First National Bank in 1888, he remained president until 1926; he also organized Carrollton's largest industry, the Mandeville Mills; a fertilizer works, a hotel, and a canning factory in Carrollton; and several industrial enterprises elsewhere.

A trustee of Agnes Scott College and Oglethorpe University, he was instrumental in obtaining the Agricultural and Mechanical School for western Georgia. The institution, opened in 1908 with a faculty of five and a student body of 110, became West Georgia College in 1933, and today has more than 7,000 students.

The Mandeville home, constructed on family property from 1889 to 1894, is replete with ornamentation in the Queen Anne style, with reeded Corinthian columns and other elements of Classical Revival style. Its turret, balconies, bay and stained-glass windows, fishscale shingles, rounded porch (now enclosed) and elaborate woodwork make it a joy to behold.

And a delightful place for a meal. Operated by the Uglum family since 1984, it has a casual, friendly atmosphere, and a wide variety of food.

Plenty of appetizers precede sandwiches (Prime Rib and Hot Chicken Salad sandwiches are unusual and popular), "Light Meals," entrée-sized salads, and heartier entrées of prime rib, Filet Mignon, Trout Almondine, and "Mix and Match" combinations from turf and surf.

Daily Specials provide great value and lots of food; Soups—Chicken Corn Chowder, Minestrone, cream of Spinach—are all homemade and tasty, and desserts are lavish.

Skip a meal sometime, and enjoy Maple Hill Pie: coffee ice cream, chocolate sauce, and sliced almonds, layered in a chocolate cookie crust.

Maple Street Mansion, 401 Maple Street, is 1 mile south of the Square; Carrollton is 50 miles west of Atlanta, 14 miles south of I-20. The restaurant is open Monday through Friday, 11:30 a.m. to 12 M, with continuous service. Saturday hours are 4 p.m. to 12 M. (404)834-2657. Dress is casual, although most men wear coat and tie at lunch; all legal beverages are available, and reservations are recommended, especially on weekends after 6 p.m. Busiest times are the end of April and first part of May, and the first 2 weeks in November. AE,MC,V, Georgia personal checks. ($$)

ITALIAN CHICKEN

1 pound dry linguine,
  cooked al dente
1½ pounds boneless,
  skinless chicken breast
Flour, seasoned with
  salt and pepper

1 cup oil
⅔ cup margarine
1½ teaspoons chopped garlic
2 Tablespoons tarragon
1 teaspoon powdered ginger

Dredge chicken in seasoned flour and cook in hot oil until brown; remove, drain, and cut into bite-sized pieces. In large skillet, heat margarine, add spices, cooked pasta, and chicken, and toss until well coated and heated through. Serves 4 to 6.

NEW YORK STRIP VERA CRUZ

Four 8-to-12-ounce strips
  cooked to desired doneness
16 ounces bottled
  picante sauce

8 ounces cheddar or
  Monterey jack cheese

On oven-proof platter, place steaks; top each with 4 ounces picante sauce, top with 2 ounces cheese, and broil until cheese melts. Serves 4.

TROUT AMANDINE

Four 8-ounce headless trout
1 cup flour, seasoned
  with salt and pepper
2 eggs
2 cups milk

¾ cup margarine, divided
4½ ounces amaretto liqueur
½ cup slivered almonds

Dredge trout in seasoned flour. In shallow bowl, beat eggs and milk together and submerge fish in mixture. In skillet, heat ½ cup margarine to medium-high; place trout skin-side up in pan, and brown 3 to 4 minutes per side. Remove and keep warm. In small pan, heat ¼ cup margarine with liqueur and almonds 2 minutes. Place trout on platter, top with almond mixture, and serve at once. Serves 4.

TWELVE SAVANNAH
Newnan

The Coweta, a tribe of the Creek Indian Nation, were based on the west bank of the Chattahoochee River; Coweta Town was above present-day Columbus. Chief William McIntosh, a Coweta and Chief of the Lower Creeks whose father was of Scottish heritage, was also an American general who fought against other tribes.

In 1805, McIntosh was a signer of the Treaty of Washington, by which the Creeks ceded lands and rights in exchange for payments of money. Many Creeks said signers of that and later treaties had no authority, and in 1824, declared any further land cessions would be punished by death.

When McIntosh signed the Treaty of Indian Springs in 1825, ceding all that remained of Georgia, he was murdered and scalped by his own people.

Coweta County, created from that cession and its later affirmation, was named for the Indian Tribe. Its seat, Newnan, was so laid out that large holdings in the county often bordered on the town, resulting in short streets, but spacious grounds surrounding some of the earlier homes.

Newnan prospered; as the center of rich agricultural country, it became a milling and textile town, and comfortable, attractive houses were built in all architectural styles during the nineteenth century.

Ella M. Leverett chose to build her quaint Victorian cottage behind an 1850s house on Greenville Street. Facing Savannah Street, near the depot and across the street from a park and bandstand, her house had numerous gables, a "gingerbread" porch, and a double parlor. It became a restaurant in 1977.

Twelve Savannah is really three restaurants in one, entered through a new, homelike section on the right. Let them know you want to be seated in the old house; it's still charming.

An enormous and unlimited buffet of traditional Southern cooking is immediately visible; separate sections provide salads, soups, five entrées (fried chicken, chicken pot pie, chicken and dumplings, barbecue from their own pit, etc., and a seafood buffet on Fridays), seven home-cooked vegetables, and homemade desserts of banana and chocolate pudding, German chocolate cake, and fruit cobblers.

"Fine Dining" from a menu of steaks, fried and broiled seafood, and combinations, is served only in the evenings. The

125

cafeteria/carryout, offering quick service, is entered from a rear door.

Many places promise "something for everyone;" Twelve Savannah delivers the goods.

Twelve Savannah, 12 Savannah Street, is open 7 days a week. Monday through Saturday, the buffet is 9 a.m. to 8 p.m., cafeteria is 10 a.m. to 9 p.m., and fine dining menu service is 5 to 8 p.m. Sunday hours are 11 a.m. to 7 p.m. (706)253-1108. Dress is "nice casual," beer and wine are available, and reservations are not necessary for groups of less than 12 unless a private room is requested. Busiest times are Mothers' Day and Powers' Crossroads Festival, Labor Day weekend. AE,DC,MC,V, Optima. ($)

HEAVENLY HASH

½ pound miniature
  marshmallows
½ pound red apples, diced
½ pound yellow apples, diced
½ cup pineapple tidbits,
  drained

2 ounces shredded coconut
1½ ounces raisins
Seedless grapes, optional
8-ounce carton sour cream

In large bowl, blend all ingredients. Serves 10 to 12.

STUFFED POTATOES

5 baking potatoes,
  washed and baked
6 ounces butter

⅓ cup sour cream
Salt and pepper
6 ounces shredded cheese

Cut potatoes in half lengthwise and remove pulp; reserve skins. In bowl, combine pulp with butter, sour cream, and seasonings. Stuff skins with mixture, top with cheese, and bake at 450 degrees until brown. Serves 10.

SWEET POTATO SOUFFLÉ

4 pounds yams, cooked soft,
    drained and peeled
2½ cups sugar
1 Tablespoon vanilla

2 eggs, beaten
4 ounces brown sugar
4 ounces raisins
1½ teaspoons cinnamon

In large bowl of mixer, blend all ingredients until smooth. Spread in greased shallow pan and bake at 350 degrees 1 hour or until done.

BANANA PUDDING

About 12 ounces
    vanilla wafers
About 6 bananas, sliced
¼ cup evaporated milk
6 Tablespoons vanilla
2½ cups sugar

4 ounces butter
About 5½ cups milk,
    divided
1 cup sifted cornstarch
Whipped cream or
    whipped topping

In large, shallow pan, spread about 8 ounces wafers; top with bananas, then remaining wafers. In large pot, mix together evaporated milk, vanilla, sugar, butter, and 4 cups milk. Bring to a boil, and immediately add 1 cup milk mixed with cornstarch. Stir well and allow to thicken; turn off heat and thin with remaining ½ cup milk, or more if required. Pour this mixture over wafers and mix well; wafers should be coated. Cover with topping and refrigerate at least one hour. Serves 10 to 12.

J. HENRY'S
Griffin

Lewis Lawrence Griffin, merchant and General in the Militia, planned the Monroe Railroad, chartered in 1833, to connect the Central Railroad at Macon with Forsyth, then with the terminus of Georgia's first two railroad lines.

That project underway, Griffin planned a second railroad, determined the point at which the two would intersect, and in 1840, sold lots to create a railroad town to be named for himself.

Before the lines were completed, however, depression caused his business to fail. Griffin, the man, left town; Griffin, the town, continued to prosper, but as a textile, rather than a railroad town. Eventually, Griffin manufacturers produced blankets, towels, velvets, velveteen, and children's socks.

Opened in 1921 on Solomon Street, two blocks west of the center of town, Dovedown Hosiery mill, the first American manufacturer of women's silk stockings to use mass-production methods, distributed its products all over the world until it ceased production in 1957.

The building was renovated in 1978 to house a mini-mall of shops and a restaurant named for one of Griffin's best-known citizens.

J. Henry Holliday was born in Griffin in 1851. During the War Between the States he contracted tuberculosis; his family moved to Valdosta, and after his mother's death, young J. Henry became a dentist and returned to Griffin to practice.

His health prompted a move to Texas, where he was known as "Doc" Holliday, gambler, gun-fighter, and all-round desperado. Despite his reputation, he died in a sanitarium in 1887, and is commemorated as a Southern gentleman of wit and charm.

He would have liked J. Henry's, and you will too. A casual, comfortable place, it is light and open, its brick walls contrasting with cream plaster and many large windows.

Food, too, is casual, but of exceptional quality and value—everything is fresh, steaks and fish are cut on the premises, and cooked to order: flat grilled, wood grilled, fried or poached.

At lunch, the "Weekday Lunch Buffet" provides a pre-set serve-yourself meal in a hurry, but there are lots of menu choices: homemade soups, quiches, omelets, and salads, plus "Lite Fare," hot entrées and generous sandwiches.

Dinner provides lots of fresh seafoods and steaks—the house specialty is Chutney Pepper Steak, flamed in brandy—and each entrée includes soup or salad and starch. Special diets can be accommodated without fuss.

Signature desserts are Rum Cream Pie and Chocolate Almond mousse pie, but you'll look a long time before you find a better pecan pie, served hot, with Vanilla Bean ice cream.

J. Henry's, 315 W. Solomon Street, is open for lunch 11:30 a.m. to 2:30 p.m., Monday through Saturday. Dinner, Monday through Thursday, is 5 to 9:30 p.m.; Friday and Saturday 5 to 10 p.m. Sunday brunch is a possibility; call for information (706)228-1762. Dress is casual, all legal beverages are available, and reservations are preferred; December is the busiest time. AE,DC,DS,MC,V, Personal checks. ($)

GRILLED ISLAND CHICKEN

½ cup rum	1 teaspoon
2 cups soy sauce	coarse-ground pepper
¼ cup brown sugar, packed	3 garlic cloves, minced
½ cup pineapple juice	2 cups olive oil
1 teaspoon whole allspice	Eight boneless,
2 teaspoons ground allspice	skinless chicken breasts

In saucepan over low heat, combine first 8 ingredients; bring to a boil, cool to room temperature, and add olive oil. Pound chicken breasts flat. In non-reactive container, marinate chicken in mixture 12 to 24 hours. Grill chicken 5 to 6 minutes on each side; serve with pineapple relish. Serves 8.

PINEAPPLE RELISH

¼ cup diced sweet red pepper	1 teaspoon olive oil
¼ cup diced sweet green pepper	¼ cup brown sugar, packed
1 teaspoon minced garlic	1 Tablespoon red wine vinegar
1 teaspoon minced scallions	1 cup fresh pineapple, diced
	1 teaspoon green peppercorns

In skillet, sauté first 4 ingredients in olive oil until soft. Stir in sugar and vinegar until dissolved. Add pineapple and peppercorns and cook 2 minutes. Remove from heat and cool to room temperature. Serve over grilled chicken or fish.

WHITE CHOCOLATE MOUSSE
with FRESH RASPBERRY SAUCE

6 ounces semi-sweet
  white chocolate
¼ teaspoon salt
4 large eggs, separated

2 teaspoons vanilla
½ cup heavy cream,
  whipped with
1½ teaspoons sugar

Combine first 2 ingredients with 2 Tablespoons hot water and melt in microwave or over hot water. Gradually stir in beaten yolks and vanilla; remove from heat. Fold in egg whites beaten to soft peaks, then whipped cream. Divide into 6 sherbet dishes and refrigerate. Serve topped with raspberry sauce.

Sauce: combine ½ cup sugar and ½ cup water in saucepan and boil until dissolved. Cool. Combine 2 ounces sugar with 1 cup fresh raspberries (or frozen raspberries without sugar) in blender or food processor and blend to smooth paste. Thin with cooled sugar syrup; strain and chill.

IN CLOVER
LaGrange

Relations between Georgia and the United States became increasingly strained during James Monroe's presidency, due to Monroe's lack of response to the state's Indian difficulties.

Creek Indians declared at their 1824 Broken Arrow council that they would never part with any more land, and the murder of Chief McIntosh by warlike Upper Creeks frightened Georgians.

Unsympathetic Indian agents hindered negotiations; Governor Troup was in open conflict with them and with new President John Quincy Adams, who disallowed the 1825 Indian Springs treaty. Troup threatened civil war, and Adams quickly corrupted Creek chiefs into ceding all lands in Georgia.

An early instance of states' rights vs. the Federal government, Troup's hollow threat (other Southern states were apathetic) was successful, and Troup County, taken from the 1826 cessions, was named for "Georgia's most fiery Governor."

When the Marquis de Lafayette visited Governor Troup in 1825, he commented on the similarity of the Creek lands to his estate, La Grange, in France. The county seat was named in his honor.

Settled by people of wealth and culture, LaGrange was, by the second half of the nineteenth century, a town of spacious homes and luxuriant gardens, surrounded by flourishing cotton plantations. It was protected by its valiant women during the War Between the States, to become a textile milling town late in the century.

Among the fine homes built during this expansion was that of Leslie Wellington Dallis, whose ownership of a woodworking company is evident in the Queen Anne-style house he built in 1892. Characterized by a hip roof with lower cross gables, decorative spindlework, and a wraparound porch, it remained in the Dallis family until 1974, when it became In Clover.

In 1988, the popular restaurant was purchased by Richard and Christina Womack, who continue to serve high quality foods, prepared and served with care. Despite the elegance of the house— be sure to take a "tour"—the atmosphere is friendly and casual.

Excellent beef and fresh seafoods are favorites here; an individual Beef Wellington is the house specialty, but there are plenty of veal and chicken dishes, plus crêpes and pastas. If you can't decide, choose a sampler platter, with the day's catch, "black and blue" chicken, and Steak Diane.

After-dinner coffees are treats, especially with homemade

desserts such as Dark Swiss Chocolate Mousse, Banana-Almond-Praline Crêpes, or Frozen Mocha Pecan Cake smothered in whipped cream.

In Clover, 205 Broad Street, is open Monday through Saturday; lunch is 11:30 a.m. to 2 p.m., and dinner 5 to 10 p.m. (706)882-0883. Dress is casual, all legal beverages are available, and reservations are accepted. AE,DC,MC,V. ($$)

SALMON MOUSSE

4 teaspoons plain gelatin
¼ teaspoon
  monosodium glutamate
1 ounce lemon juice
1½ teaspoons paprika
½ cup finely chopped celery

½ cup finely
  chopped cucumber
15-ounce can salmon,
  carefully picked over
1½ cups mayonnaise
1 hard cooked egg, chopped

In small bowl, soak gelatin in ½ cup cold water; add 2 cups boiling water. Pour into blender with seasonings and vegetables; mix well. In another bowl, flake salmon, mix with mayonnaise and egg, and stir in gelatin mixture. Divide mousse among 12 6-ounce molds coated with vegetable spray. Refrigerate. Unmold to serve 12.

LACE COOKIES

1 cup butter (no substitute)
1 pound light brown sugar
2¼ cups
  quick-cooking oatmeal

3 Tablespoons flour
1 teaspoon salt
1 egg, beaten
1 teaspoon vanilla

In 2-quart pan, melt butter, add brown sugar and stir. Blend in remaining ingredients. Drop by LEVEL measuring teaspoon onto buttered non-stick cookie sheets and bake at 375 degrees about 5 minutes, until golden brown. Cool 30 seconds; remove with spatula onto racks. If cookies mash, they are too warm; if they stick or break, they are too cool and need reheating. May be stored in air-tight containers in freezer. Yields 10 dozen.

FROZEN MOCHA PECAN CAKE

24 chocolate wafer cookies,
  crumbled (1½ cups)
¼ cup sugar
¼ cup melted margarine
8-ounce package
  cream cheese, softened
14-ounce can sweetened
  condensed milk

⅔ cup chocolate syrup
2 Tablespoons
  instant coffee
1 cup heavy cream,
  whipped
1 cup chopped pecans

In bowl, combine crumbs, sugar, and margarine. Pat crumbs firmly on bottom and sides of buttered 9" springform pan OR 9" x 13" pan; chill. In large bowl of mixer, whip cheese and add condensed milk and chocolate syrup. In cup, dissolve coffee in 1 teaspoon hot water; blend into mixture. Fold in whipped cream. Pour ½ mixture into pan, sprinkle with ⅔ of pecans, add remaining mixture, then remaining pecans in decorative ring on top. Cover and freeze at least 6 hours. Garnish each serving with additional crumbs and whipped cream if desired. Store in freezer.

THE BULLOCH HOUSE
RESTAURANT
Warm Springs

Wounded Native American warriors made their way to springs of warm water and soft mud near Pine Mountain; here, protected by the Spirit who heated the waters, they immersed themselves in the healing springs.

The warm springs were discovered by a group of Savannahians fleeing a late-eighteenth-century fever epidemic, and fame of the healthful waters predated the Creek Indians' 1826 cession of the land to Georgia. By 1832, a village had grown up around the springs.

Destroyed by accidental fire in the late 1860s, the rebuilt resort was a fashionable watering place toward the end of the nineteenth century, attracting visitors from all over the South.

In the little town of Durand, Georgia, Benjamin F. Bulloch decided to relocate his dry-goods store to a more profitable area; according to family tradition, in 1891, the building was rolled on logs 4.5 miles, to the railroad junction where visitors to the springs deboarded. The town of Bullochsville grew up across the railroad tracks from the warm springs, and Bulloch built an impressive house on a hill overlooking his town.

With its sloping hip roof, turreted dormer, fishscale-shingled gable, paired columns, and ballustraded, wrap-around porch, it incorporates elements of the most popular styles of its time. The house remained in the Bulloch family until purchased by its present owners in 1990, although it had stood empty for five years, and was in need of serious repair.

New owners Judy Foster, her brother Charles Garrett, and his wife Sylvia engaged a craftsman, a Bulloch descendant, to help restore the house and add a banquet room, and the Bulloch House Restaurant was opened in December, 1990.

High-ceilinged large rooms with beaded wainscots are painted yellow, rose, and dark green, reflecting colors in chintz swags over windows. Ceiling fans and double doors enhance the open, "Old South" feeling of generous hospitality.

An expansion of their earlier restaurant in nearby Manchester, the new restaurant's food is "like Grandmother's": homemade biscuits and corn bread, with local vegetables and REAL mashed potatoes—at least 100 pounds a day—accompanying their famous fried chicken and other Southern favorites.

Chicken pie, with chunks of chicken—just chicken—between two layers of hand-rolled crust, has to be tried to be believed; there's often ham and potato pie; chicken and dumplings; roast beef, cooked all night in its own gravy; and roast turkey and dressing once a week, all year 'round.

Buffet offerings change daily, but there are always two meats, four vegetables, and two salad bars, and you can call for a recorded list each day. Menu items include grilled marinated chicken, homemade chicken salad plate, burgers, and sandwiches, with steaks and catfish in the evening.

Among special desserts are chocolate, coconut, and chocolate-chip pecan pies, homemade cheesecake and fruit cobblers, and old-fashioned yellow cake with thick caramel frosting. Occasionally you'll find fried fruit pies, tea cakes (cookies, to the uninitiated), and Judy's incredible Butter Roll, a buttery, sugary pastry topped with a slow-simmered custard sauce.

The Bulloch House is on US 27A and GA 41, just south of town. Lunch, 7 days a week, is 11 a.m. to 2:30 p.m.; dinner, Thursday through Saturday, is 5:30 to 8:30 p.m. (706)665-9068; 665-9057 for recording of day's menu. Dress is casual, reservations are accepted except for Easter, Mother's Day, etc., and the busiest time is during December. Credit cards are not accepted; personal checks accepted. ($)

CORN BREAD

1¾ cups self-rising corn meal   ¾ cup vegetable shortening
3 eggs   2 cups buttermilk

In large bowl, place meal and make a well in center. Blend eggs with shortening; using hands, mix into meal, gradually adding buttermilk. Pour into greased 9" x 13" pan, and bake at 450 degrees 12 to 15 minutes, or until nicely browned and springs back when touched.

CANDIED YAMS

4 cups sugar   8 cups sliced
2 cups water   fresh sweet potatoes

In large pot, bring sugar and water to rolling boil. Add sweet potatoes and cook over medium heat until tender. Excellent with turnip greens! Serves about 16.

RAISIN SAUCE FOR BAKED HAM

16 ounces pineapple juice   ¼ cup honey
½ cup brown sugar   .   ½ cup water
2 Tablespoons mustard   ¼ cup corn starch
                                  1¼ cups raisins

In large saucepan, bring first 4 ingredients to boil. Mix water with corn starch and pour into boiling mixture. Add raisins and simmer 10 minutes. If not thick enough, add more corn starch by same method. Serve warm over sliced baked ham or pass separately. Yields about 3½ cups.

VICTORIAN TEA ROOM
Warm Springs

Visitors of all sorts were welcomed to the springs and Bullochsville: invalids, social Southerners, and, in 1924, a future President of the United States.

Struck by infantile paralysis (polio) in 1921, Franklin Roosevelt exercised in the warm waters, and was so benefitted that he returned frequently, often bringing other patients.

Bullochsville and the springs consolidated in 1924, and Warm Springs became well known during the Roosevelt years as home of "The Little White House."

After the President's death there in 1945, Warm Springs declined, despite a brief attempt to make it a Western-style tourist attraction. In 1983, three enterprising women, Jean Kidd, June Jones, and Carolyn Cranford, bought what they call "half a town," and began its revitalization.

They spent a year cleaning, painting, and repairing, opening twenty-six shops in 1984; by December, 1991, there were sixty-five shops and seven restaurants in Warm Springs. In the past, there were perhaps twenty-five visitors per day, primarily to the Little White House museum; now, they average six hundred daily, twice the number of the residents.

One of the partners, June Jones, had owned a tea room in Columbus, and, with her brother, Oscar Rumsey, opened The Victorian Tea Room in Warm Springs. Rapidly growing, they moved into the tall building next door in 1986. Built in 1906 as Talbott's General Mercantile, it had been an opera house during the western period; the two-story colonnaded porch dates from this time.

The high beaded ceiling, painted dark green, sets the color scheme of green, rose, and buff, with country artifacts and brass displayed on high shelves. Below, lovingly prepared, generously served Southern home-cooked food refreshes the weary tourist.

Here you'll find hearty soups—black bean, beef vegetable, Brunswick stew—varied salads— chunky chicken salad with nuts and apples, taco salad, and crisp greens topped with grilled chicken—plus burgers, sandwiches, and a daily hot lunch menu. Especially popular is "Lunch in a Basket," of soup, sandwich, and dessert.

Saturday and Sunday buffets always offer Southern fried chicken, with baked ham, sweet and sour meat loaf, and other favorites rotating. Notable vegetables include Hopping John, fresh collard greens, creamed corn, steamed cabbage, home-grown pole beans, and squash casserole.

If you're lucky, one of the dessert offerings will be French Silk Pie: dark, rich, covered with whipped cream and chocolate shavings, all on a flaky, tender crust.

The Victorian Tea Room, Broad Street, Warm Springs, is open for lunch 7 days a week, 11:30 a.m. to 3 p.m., seasonally until 6 or 7 p.m. on Saturday. It is closed on Monday in January and February. (706)655-2319. Dress is casual, wine and beer are available, and reservations are accepted only for parties of 15 or more. Busiest times are Christmas Candlelight Tour, the weekend before Thanksgiving, and Spring Fling, 3rd weekend in April. MC,V. ($)

CHICKEN AND RICE SOUP*

3-pound chicken, washed
3 stalks celery, chopped
1 large onion, chopped
¾ cup rice, washed well
28-ounce can whole tomatoes, chopped, with juice
Salt and pepper

In large pot, cover chicken with water and bring to a boil. Cover and reduce heat; simmer until tender. Remove chicken and cool; strain broth, add vegetables, return to boil, then reduce heat and cook until tender. In another pot, cover rice with water, bring to boil, then simmer 10 minutes. Cover, remove from heat, and let stand 15 minutes. Add rice to soup. Skin and debone chicken, leaving in large pieces. Add to soup, with tomatoes and juice. Season and serve hot. Serves 8.

SQUASH CASSEROLE*

2 pounds yellow squash, sliced
1 medium onion, sliced
¼ green pepper, chopped
2-ounce jar diced pimiento
2 eggs, beaten
1 cup grated cheddar cheese
½ cup mayonnaise
2 Tablespoons margarine or butter
Salt and red pepper
Grated cheese for topping

In large saucepan, cook squash and onion in small amount water until tender. Drain. Add remaining ingredients and mix well. Pour into 3-quart baking dish, sprinkle with additional cheese, and bake at 350 degrees until browned. Serves 6 to 8.

LEMON ICE BOX PIE*

9-inch graham cracker
  pie crust, baked
14-ounce can sweetened
  condensed milk

3 eggs, separated
Juice of 3 lemons
Dash cream of tartar
6 Tablespoons sugar

In bowl, combine condensed milk with egg yolks; add lemon juice slowly and mix well. Pour into crust. In large bowl of mixer, whip egg whites with cream of tartar; add sugar gradually. Spread over top of pie; place pie under broiler and lightly brown, watching constantly. Refrigerate and serve cold.

*From *Victorian Tea Room Favorite Recipes*, Warm Springs, Georgia. Copyright © 1991. Used by permission.

BLUDAU'S
AT THE 1839 GOETCHIUS HOUSE
Columbus

The Federal Road, authorized by Congress in 1805, connected Washington City with New Orleans by a much shorter route than the Great Valley Road west to Nashville, then the Natchez Trace south.

It traversed present-day Georgia in a westerly direction from Augusta to the Chattahoochee River. Much of the land belonged to Creek Indians, but by the Treaty of Washington of 1805, they ceded land between the Oconee and Ocmulgee rivers, plus the right-of-way for a horse path to Mobile.

There were six rivers to cross on the rough track through the wilderness, and "houses of entertainment" were exorbitant, filthy, and insect-ridden. Still, hundreds made the trip, three stage lines competed for their business, and the various crossings of the Chattahoochee finally became one, the state-planned town of Columbus.

Laid out after the 1826 treaty with the Creeks, Columbus grew rapidly; a traveler in 1833 described five hotels and a population of 1,000. Six years later, architect-builder Richard Rose Goetchius, a New Yorker of Dutch extraction, built a New-Orleans style Greek Revival house for his Southern bride.

Unlike any other structures in the area, the low, sprawling house has a full width gallery, a magnificent doorway with stained-glass transom and sidelights, and tiny windows and heavy Italianate brackets beneath its eaves.

The Goetchius house remained in the family until 1969, although rented as doctors' offices after 1924. Placed on the National Register in 1969, it was cut into seven sections and moved eight blocks that same year to the historic district on the banks of the Chattahoochee.

Reproduction iron lace and plasterwork replaced that removed or damaged in the move, and is hardly detectable.

Adapted for use as a restaurant, it is operated by Werner Bludau, a Swiss. Bludau's at the 1839 Goetchius House is gracious and welcoming, decorated with appropriate antiques. Fresh flowers and candlelight are reflected in tall windows, and Bludau's classic Continental cuisine features fresh Southern ingredients, prepared with skill and care.

Seafood, beef, and lamb are all hand cut and trimmed, and whole fish are cut into steaks and filets in the kitchen. Fresh veal, lamb, and duckling are used in several classic dishes each.

145

You might begin your meal with an appetizer of steamed mussels in the shell, classic Coquilles St. Jacques, or Charleston "She" Crab Soup. After a satisfying entrée, take time to study the dessert tray: perhaps there's White Chocolate Mousse Cake, enveloped in dark chocolate; Grand Marnier layer cake; or freshly made cheesecake, topped with strawberries and blueberries. You can't go wrong!

Bludau's at the 1839 Goetchius House, 405 Broadway, is open for dinner 5:30 to 9:45 p.m., Monday through Thursday, until 10:45 p.m. Friday and Saturday. (706)324-4863. Dress is "nice casual up," all legal beverages are available, and reservations are requested, especially for parties of 6 or more. AE,DC,DS,MC,V. ($$$)

VEAL MAISON

2 pounds veal tenderloin
Flour
3 egg yolks, beaten
Butter
13-ounce can artichoke hearts
1 medium sweet green pepper,
 in ¼" slivers
½ medium onion,
 in ¼" slivers

Heaping Tablespoon
 garlic butter
⅓ cup Sauterne or white wine
¼ cup diced pimiento
Large pinch each tarragon
leaves, salt, and thyme
Grated cheddar cheese
Grated Swiss cheese
Pecan halves

Cut veal into medallions; pound until tender. Dredge in flour, then dip in beaten yolks. In large sauté pan, melt butter and sauté, in batches, 30 seconds on each side. Set aside. In same pan, sauté next 6 ingredients with seasonings, tossing 3 to 4 minutes. Divide veal onto six ovenproof plates, spoon vegetables over, sprinkle with grated cheeses and top with pecans. Place in 400 degree oven until cheese melts. Serves 6.

ROAST DUCKLING WITH PECAN STUFFING

1 cup finely chopped onion
1 cup finely chopped carrot
1 cup finely chopped celery
1 cup chopped
  seedless raisins, optional
¼ cup sherry
3 Tablespoons
  red currant jelly

1 cup finely chopped pecans
1 egg, beaten
4 cups soft bread crumbs
Two 2½ pound ducks
Worcestershire sauce
Black pepper
Rosemary leaves

In roasting pan, combine first four ingredients; roast in 350 degree oven until browned, stirring often. Stir in next five ingredients, and stuff ducks with mixture. Brush ducks with Worcestershire sauce, sprinkle with pepper and rosemary leaves, and roast at 325 degrees about 20 minutes per pound, or until desired doneness. Split ducks lengthwise. Serves 4.

BEALL'S 1860
Macon

Prehistoric Indians, who farmed the land where the fall line crosses the Ocmulgee River, built enormous ceremonial mounds there about 900 A.D., then disappeared. Later inhabitants, forerunners of the Creek Indians, saw Spaniards with de Soto come through.

Fort Hawkins, the area's first European outpost, was built in 1806. Here, troops were mustered and sent to General Jackson before the Battle of New Orleans in the War of 1812.

Macon was laid out in 1823, planned by the State as a trading town. General Lafayette thought it already a "handsome village" when he visited in 1825.

An inland port, Macon was linked by flatboats with the Eastern Seaboard, and prospered from the beginning; steamboats and railroads assured its future.

By 1860, Macon had 7,000 people, three railroads, and a women's college, and wealthy citizens built their imposing houses on hills above town. Nathan Beall did not long enjoy his Italianate house on College Hill; his plantation was destroyed by Sherman's army, the cotton market, on which Macon's economy was based, collapsed, and the house was sold for $30 thousand in 1865.

Leonidas Jordan, capitalist, planter, and proprietor of Macon's Academy of Music, spent $100 thousand remodeling the house in 1895, creating the vaulted entrance hall and dining room, and adding columns on three sides.

His widow sold the house to her brother in 1906, when she married John Little of Atlanta. She left a trust fund to build the Ilah Dunlap Little Memorial Library at the University of Georgia, specifying that it, too, must be surrounded by columns.

The house remained in the Dunlap family until 1940, then the Lassiter family made it an elegant boarding house until 1961. As the Lassiter House, it was placed on the National Register in 1972.

During later ownership, periods of vacancy alternated with injudicious remodeling until John Hanberry purchased it in 1980. Named for its builder, Beall's 1860 is returning the house to its period of elegance.

It is bright and open at lunch, when Chicken Sweet and Hot (boneless breast, marinated and served in red currant jelly-horseradish sauce) and Grilled Chicken Salad are popular, and a 30-item salad bar fills the tile stove alcove in the former dining room.

149

Beautifully lighted inside and out, Beall's makes an event of dinner. Breads are baked fresh daily, homemade soups—Steak and Vegetable, Patio Tomato—are outstanding, and fresh seafoods are emphasized, although the house specialty, prime rib (in three sizes), is the favorite.

Among desserts, homemade Chocolate Walnut Pie outsells others three-to-one, but it's hard to resist Mud Pie, built of mocha and rocky road ice creams on a cookie crust, topped with chocolate frosting, pecans and whipped cream.

Beall's 1860, 315 College Street, is open Monday through Friday for lunch, 11:30 a.m. to 2:30 p.m. Dinner, Monday through Saturday, is 5 to 10 p.m. The restaurant is open on certain holidays—Easter, Mothers' Day, etc. (912)745-3663. All legal beverages are available, dress is casual, although half the men wear coat and tie, and reservations are preferred, especially for parties of 6 or more. Busiest time is Cherry Blossom Festival, the 3rd week in March. AE,DC,DS,MC,V. ($$)

PEANUT SOUP

4 cups chicken stock
1 onion, peeled and chopped
2 stalks celery, chopped

2 cups half and half cream
3 cups peanut butter
Chopped peanuts

In large pot, cook stock with vegetables; strain, return to pot, add cream and peanut butter. Serve hot with chopped nuts sprinkled on top. This is very rich; yields about 10 small servings.

TURKEY DIVAN

2 pounds broccoli, steamed
1 cup grated Parmesan cheese
2 pounds chopped or
   pulled cooked turkey
10-ounce can
   cream of chicken soup

¾ cup sour cream
¾ cup mayonnaise
1 Tablespoon lemon juice
1 teaspoon curry powder
Salt and pepper

In baking dish, distribute steamed broccoli; sprinkle with ½ Parmesan cheese, then turkey, then remaining cheese. In bowl, blend remaining ingredients; spread mixture over turkey. Heat at 350 degrees 35-40 minutes or until browned and bubbling. Serves 6 to 8.

RUM CAKE

1 cup chopped pecans
18½-ounce box
 Duncan Hines™
 Golden Butter Cake mix
3¾-ounce package instant
 vanilla pudding mix

4 eggs
½ cup light rum
½ cup water
½ cup vegetable oil
Glaze*

Grease and flour large tube pan. Sprinkle nuts on bottom of pan. In large bowl of mixer, mix dry ingredients, then add liquids. Beat 3 minutes; pour into pan and bake at 325 degrees 50-60 minutes. Pour hot glaze over cake and leave one hour before removing from pan.

*Glaze: in saucepan, melt 1 stick butter with 1 cup sugar. Remove from heat and stir in ½ cup light rum.

THE NEW PERRY HOTEL
Perry

Early maps of Georgia show the western boundary extending to the Mississippi River, although the land, occupied by Creek Indians, was claimed by Spain until 1795, when the United States created the Territory of Mississippi. In exchange for a promise to remove the Creeks, Georgia renounced her claims in 1802; nineteen years passed before lands between the Ocmulgee and Flint rivers were obtained.

Houston (pronounced "house-ton") County, laid out in 1821, finally opened up more of the rich Middle Georgia farmland. Settlers rushed to claim it, and the county seat, Perry, incorporated in 1824, was named for Commodore Perry, hero of the Battle of Lake Erie.

By 1849, a stagecoach line extended south to Perry from the east-west Federal Road at Macon, and Cox's Inn accommodated overnight guests. Its successor, The Perry Hotel, was built in 1870, when the Southwestern Railroad (now the Central of Georgia) opened a line from Fort Valley to Perry.

The large, two-story wooden hotel was demolished in 1924, making way for the NEW Perry Hotel, completed the following year. A popular stop for Florida-bound tourists from the 1920s, when US 41 was paved, the New Perry Hotel has been owned and operated by the same family since 1944.

Carefully maintained, the 3-story Georgian structure shows few changes, although the portico's ground level was enclosed when deteriorating columns were replaced about 1960. Grounds are spacious, filled at all seasons with blooming plants, and hospitality is still dispensed with a lavish hand.

Entered through a home-like lobby decorated with fresh flowers, the dining room of the New Perry Hotel is justly famed. Surrounded by botanical drawings of camellias, guests enjoy traditional Southern cuisine, prepared by long-time employees.

Chicken is a favorite, whether Southern fried, pan-broiled (with dressing), or in crusty old-fashioned Chicken Pan Pie. Dinners of spring lamb chops, grilled or fried farm-raised catfish, roast beef and steaks vary daily, and include soup, relish, three vegetables, and a choice of salads, plus homemade corn sticks you'll long remember.

Pecan and lemon chess pies are outstanding, but seasonal "pan pie" is not to be missed: apple, blackberry, or peach, generously scooped out with chunks of flaky crust, topped with whipped cream.

The New Perry Hotel is on US 41, US 341, and I-75 Business Loop. (912)987-1000. Dining Room is open 7 days a week; breakfast is 7 to 10 a.m., lunch is 11:30 a.m. to 2:30 p.m., and dinner is 5:30 to 9 p.m. Dress is casual, and reservations are not required. Busiest times are special holidays. There are 56 overnight units. AE,MC,V. ($)

CHEESE SOUFFLÉ

1 tube saltine crackers,
  crushed
4 eggs, beaten
1½ cups shredded
  sharp cheese

⅓ cup melted butter
3 cups milk
Salt and pepper

In bowl, mix all ingredients well. Pour into greased 1½ quart baking dish. Bake at 350 degrees about 45 minutes, or until toothpick comes out clean.

SWEET POTATO CASSEROLE

6 medium sweet potatoes,
  cooked and mashed
½ cup pineapple juice
3 eggs, beaten

½ cup margarine
1 cup sugar
Dash nutmeg
Topping*

In bowl, mix all ingredients well. Pour into greased baking dish, bake at 350 degrees 45 minutes; crumble topping on potatoes and bake 5 minutes more.

*For topping, stir together: 1 cup brown sugar, packed; ⅓ cup flour; 1 cup shredded coconut; 1 cup chopped nuts.

CURRIED FRUIT

⅓ cup butter
¾ cup brown sugar, packed
2 Tablespoons
  curry powder
1-pound can pineapple
  chunks, drained
  (reserve ¼ cup juice)

1-pound can peach halves,
  drained and sliced
1-pound can pear halves,
  drained and sliced
10 maraschino cherries,
  halved

In skillet, melt butter, add sugar and curry and stir in juice. Mix well and simmer. Pour fruit into buttered shallow 1½-quart baking dish; pour hot sauce over, and bake at 350 degrees about 1 hour. Serves 8.

PEACH PAN PIE

Prepared short-crust pastry
¼ cup water
1 cup sugar

3 cups sliced fresh peaches
Butter
Flour

In large pan, bring water and sugar to boil; add peaches and simmer briefly. Line sides of baking dish with pastry; lift out peaches and layer in dish, alternating with dots of butter and sprinkles of flour. Cover with top crust, slashed. Bake at 350 degrees 45 minutes, or until top crust is browned.

THE BLACK SWAN INN
Hawkinsville

Wh
hen Pulaski County was formed in 1808, lands west of the Ocmulgee River still belonged to Creek Indians, who had only recently vacated lands ceded in 1802 and 1805. Hartford, the county seat, was established on the east bank of the Ocmulgee in an attempt to prevent their return; the site chosen had been an Indian trading place.

After later Indian cessions, a town grew up on the bluff on the west bank. It was named for Colonel Benjamin Hawkins, the "Beloved Man of the Four Nations" of Creek Indians, who had been a fair and helpful agent over all Indians south of the Ohio River.

Hawkinsville grew much more rapidly than Hartford, and in 1837, when it was incorporated as the new county seat, many buildings in Hartford were dismantled and moved across the river.

The trading center of a thriving agricultural area, Hawkinsville's industries included the ginning of cotton. Its transportation on the then-navigable Ocmulgee was big business— seven steamboats and 60 towboats plied the river in 1836—and greatly improved the town's economy.

James Pope Brown, cotton planter, hotel owner, and politician, moved into his elegant new home about 1906. The two-story Neoclassical frame house is dominated by an unusual full-height porch and a lower full-width porch, each supported by paired columns and topped with a balustraded balcony.

No expense was spared in its construction; transom and sidelights of both front doors are of beveled and leaded glass, rooms are spacious, and the wide entrance hall, set off by columns, features a soaring staircase.

Brown lived in the house only three years; a succession of owners followed, and in 1985, local business investors purchased the house and renovated it to become a restaurant/bed and breakfast inn, filling a long-time need in Hawkinsville.

Beautifully decorated in soft pastels, the Black Swan Inn is named for the last steamboat on the Ocmulgee. It is the perfect spot for a pleasant lunch, a romantic dinner, or a weekend stay while enjoying spring races in the "Harness Horse Capital of Georgia."

Lunch might begin with Tomato Basil Soup, or, in warm weather, Cold Cantaloupe Soup, followed by homemade tuna, chicken, or ham salad, or a croissant sandwich. At dinner, the

157

cuisine is Continental, and choice rib eye is grilled with garlic-parsley butter; scallops are sautéed with lime-ginger butter, and breast of chicken simmered with mushrooms, onions, and wine; the evening's special might be quail stuffed with wild rice, sauced with wine.

Desserts, at any time, are memorable: Margarita cheesecake and Irish Cream cheesecake in rich crumb crusts, classic Bananas Foster, homemade lemon sherbet, and Decadent Chocolate Cake, served with crème fraîche.

The Black Swan Inn, 411 Progress Avenue, is open for lunch Monday, Tuesday, and Wednesday, 11:30 a.m. to 1:30 p.m., and for dinner Monday through Saturday, 6 to 10 p.m. (912)783-4466. Dress is casual, although most men wear jackets, wine and imported beers are available, and reservations are suggested. There are 6 overnight units. AE,DC,MC,V. ($$)

PETITE PALACE PASTA

1 pound fettuccine, cooked al dente	2 ounces olive oil
	4 tomatoes, quartered
1 pound chicken livers	2 ounces balsamic vinegar
½ cup flour	2 ounces chicken stock
1 teaspoon paprika	2 ounces dry red wine
	1 teaspoon rosemary leaves

Clean and rinse livers. Dredge in flour mixed with paprika. In large sauté pan, heat oil; sauté livers until brown. Add remaining ingredients and reduce until thickened. Serve over hot fettuccine. Serves 4.

VEAL SCALLOPPINE

2 veal cutlets
⅛ cup flour
2 ounces butter

2 ounces prosciutto
2 ounces Parmesan cheese
½ cup white wine
½ teaspoon ground sage

Dredge veal in flour. In sauté pan, heat butter and sauté veal until brown. Remove from pan; on top of each cutlet, place prosciutto, then cheese, and broil until brown. Reheat pan juices with wine and sage; reduce until of sauce consistency. Pour over veal and serve. Serves 2.

THE WINDSOR HOTEL
Americus

Creek Indian corn crops attested to the richness of land along Muckalee Creek, and Americus, seat of Sumpter County, was founded in 1832 on the site of the "granary of the Creek Nation."

Many people in Americus believed it could become a winter resort for wealthy Northerners, and in 1890, local investors contributed $100,000 to construct a hotel.

Designed by Atlanta Architect G.L. Norman in "Whimsical Victorian" style, the Windsor Hotel, named for one of its investors, is a brick edifice of three and five stories, ornamented with arches, turrets, cupolas, and balconies. Elements of many styles are incorporated, but the overall impression is of Richardsonian Romanesque.

The tourists did not materialize; guests were primarily regular commercial travelers, and the hotel changed hands several times, closing in 1974.

As part of the Americus Historic District, it was placed on the National Register in 1976, and in 1986, a group of local investors—many of them descendants of the original group—joined forces to restore it.

The Windsor reopened in 1991, after a meticulous $5 million renovation, and the second-floor dining room is again known for delicious meals.

Regional Southern cuisine is featured on the lunchtime buffet, with a choice of soups (cold melon, peach, or gazpacho in hot weather), six vegetables and two starches, two hot meats, and a build-your-own sandwich table of meats, cheeses, etc. Juicy fruit cobblers are next to an enormous silver bowl of serve-yourself ice cream, or you can make a sundae with half a dozen toppings. A menu is available for those who want a sandwich or light meal.

Dinner at the Windsor leans to lighter Continental and regional cuisine, changing seasonally: in the fall, perhaps grilled quail with apple butter, or salmon with cabernet and dill butter. Summer might bring grilled chicken with tarragon-mustard glaze, or pannéed trout in bourbon-mushroom sauce.

Whether your choice is a light healthful meal or a rich desert, it will be beautifully prepared and served with flair in one of Georgia's most outstanding buildings.

Pack your bags and make a reservation.

The Grand Dining Room of the Windsor Hotel is open 7 days a week; breakfast is 6:30 to 10:30 a.m., lunch is 11:30 a.m. to 2 p.m., and dinner is 5:30 to 9:30 p.m. (912)924-1555. Dress is casual, although most men wear coat and tie at lunch, all legal beverages are available (except Sunday) and reservations are recommended. Parties of 12 or more will be seated in a private dining room. There are 53 overnight units. AE,CB,DS,MC,V. ($$)

AUTUMN PUMPKIN BISQUE

2 pounds pumpkin, peeled,
   in 1" cubes
1 pound bacon, diced
1 medium onion, diced fine
½ teaspoon cumin

¼ cup chopped parsley
4 cups half and half cream
Salt and pepper
1½ cups grated Gruyère
   or Swiss cheese

In large pot over low heat, sweat pumpkin in small amount of water 40 minutes; test for tenderness. Remove from heat and cool slightly; mash and set aside. In the pot, render bacon over medium heat. Add onion and sauté until translucent. Combine with pumpkin pulp and stir in remaining ingredients except cheese. Simmer until slightly thickened. Divide into bowls and top with cheese. Serves 12.

BREAST OF CHICKEN
WITH MORELS AND BLACKBERRY SAUCE

6 boneless chicken breasts
Butter
12 ounces morels OR
   other mushrooms, chopped
⅓ cup minced shallot
½ teaspoon thyme

Seasoned flour
¼ cup Madeira or Port
½ cup blackberry brandy
2 cups Brown Sauce or
   rich gravy
Sour cream for garnish

162

Loosen skin on chicken, being careful not to break it. In large skillet, melt butter and sauté mushrooms, shallots, and thyme until aroma begins to arise from pan. Cool. Stuff mushroom mixture under skin of chicken. Dredge breasts in flour, place in skillet, and sauté over medium heat until golden. Remove to shallow pan and cook at 350 degrees 12 to 15 minutes. Deglaze skillet with wine and brandy. Flame, add Brown Sauce, and simmer until lightly thickened. Distribute sauce on 6 dinner plates. With decorating bag and fine tip, pipe swirls of sour cream into sauce. Place breasts on sauce and serve. Serves 6.

BREAST OF DUCKLING
WITH STRAWBERRIES AND PEPPERCORNS

Six 10-ounce
  boneless duck breasts
⅛ cup Riesling
¼ cup chicken stock

Salt and pepper
3 Tablespoons
  green peppercorns
12 fresh strawberries, sliced
¼ cup strawberry jam

Cut slashes into skin and fat of each breast. In large sauté pan, cook ducks, skin-side down, over medium-high heat until fully browned. Pour off excess fat; turn breasts and reduce heat. Add wine and stock and cook to desired doneness. Remove duck from pan; rest a few minutes, then slice thinly from top and fan on 6 warm plates. Add remaining ingredients to pan, simmer 1 minute and pour over breasts. Serves 6.

RADIUM SPRINGS LODGE RESTAURANT
near Albany

Prehistoric Indians visited a group of cold, blue-water springs near the Flint River more than two thousand years ago; archaeological remains indicate they may have had a village nearby. Creek Indians called it "Skywater," believing the water had magical and curative powers.

The largest natural spring in Georgia, it has a constant temperature of 68 degrees, and the water rises under pressure through a circular opening in solid limestone at a rate of 70 thousand gallons per minute.

Early settlers named it "Blue Springs," but when the water was tested in the 1920s, it was determined to have more radium than most spas, and the name was changed to reflect this content.

At the center of a development that included two golf courses, horseback riding, canoeing, and a glamorous casino, Radium Springs was a popular resort. A hunting lodge built about 1912 housed overnight visitors; in the 1960s, it became a restaurant, renovated and reopened by Charles and Han Finley in 1990.

Restoration of the casino in 1992 readied it for banquets and receptions; lunch is a possibility. The spring, long unused, was reopened for public swimming in summer, 1992, and other buildings on the property are scheduled for renovation.

Radium Springs Lodge Restaurant, nestled in a grove of mossy trees, is an oasis of fine food. Han Finley brings her German background, and John King, his Northern experience, to create a Southern variation on New American Cuisine that'll knock your socks off. Specializing in fresh Gulf seafoods and hand-cut beef, veal, and lamb, they prepare each order from scratch, using healthful products; a veal dish prepared for a special diet has become a popular entrée.

Creative pairing of sauces with entrées produces entirely new flavors: grouper is grilled with mango chutney/pecan sauce; shrimp and scallops sautéed with Stilton are served on angelhair pasta; and Southwestern shrimp combines all the best flavors from that region.

For a traditional touch, German Schnitzel is served with potato pancakes, sautéed cabbage and apples, and "she" crab soup is made from an old Carolina receipt.

"Sweet conclusions" are all you could desire, especially the Snicker Pie in which chocolate, caramel, and peanuts are layered over cream cheese in a graham cracker crust.

Radium Springs Lodge Restaurant, 2511 Radium Springs Road, is about 3 miles south of Albany, just west of US 19. It is open Tuesday through Saturday, 5:30 to 10 p.m. (912)883-3871. Dress is casual, all legal beverages are available, and reservations, not required, are suggested on weekends and for parties of 6 or more. AE,MC,V. ($$)

RED PEPPER JELLY

1 large sweet red pepper	1½ cups sugar
1 large jalapeño pepper	1 cup white vinegar
	1½ Tablespoons plain gelatin

In blender or food processor, purée peppers. Combine in saucepan with vinegar, and boil 3 minutes. Remove from heat and rest 20 minutes. Finely strain to remove skin and seeds. Boil 3 minutes, stir in gelatin, cool and store in jars. Jelly will be solid when cold, but melts rapidly. Use on blackened foods and seafood that tends to be dry, such as tuna or swordfish. Yields about 1½ cups.

BLACKENING SPICE

1 Tablespoon granulated garlic	1½ teaspoons thyme
1½ teaspoons oregano	1½ teaspoons granulated onion
1 Tablespoon white pepper	2 teaspoons seasoning salt
1½ teaspoons cayenne	6 Tablespoons paprika

In bowl, mix all spices until well blended. To use, brush steak, chicken, or seafood with butter and generously coat one side with blackening spice. Brush hot grill with butter, place item spice-side down, brush top with butter and coat with spice. Grill each side until done. Yields about ¾ cup.

CURRY SAUCE FOR POACHED SALMON

½ cup sour cream
½ cup mayonnaise
1 teaspoon
    creamed horseradish
½ teaspoon (or to taste)
    curry powder

2 ounces Florida crab
    claw meat
Chopped fresh dill
    for garnish

In bowl, blend all ingredients well. Sauce may be served warm or chilled over salmon; garnish sauce with dill. Yields about 1½ cups.

MANGO CHUTNEY PECAN SAUCE

1 to 2 Tablespoons butter
½ cup chopped pecans
½ medium sweet
    red pepper, diced
3 scallions, diced

8-ounce jar Major Grey
    mango chutney
1 ounce prepared honey-
    mustard salad dressing

In sauté pan, melt enough butter to cover bottom of pan; over low heat, slowly roast pecans until hot. Add remaining ingredients and heat over low heat until mixture begins to bubble. Remove from heat and store chilled. May be served either hot or cold; especially good with grilled seafood, beef, and pork entrées. Yields about 1½ cups.

STATESBORO INN
AND RESTAURANT
Statesboro

Although Bulloch County was created in 1796, no county seat was chosen until 1801, when 200 acres were donated by a wealthy landowner. Laid out at an existing crossroads, Statesboro was finally founded in 1806, but growth was slow, and there were only a few residents by mid-century.

During Sherman's "March to the Sea," Union foragers near the village were overtaken by Confederate cavalry on December 4, 1864. In the resulting skirmish, 27 Federals were captured; the rest escaped to their main force, which drove off the Confederates.

With the way to Savannah clear before them, two divisions of the Federal 15th Corps camped overnight.

By 1880, Statesboro still had only 25 people, but it soon became the largest inland exporter of Sea Island cotton, and it grew rapidly from the 1890s to the 1920s.

William G. Raines' hardware store also prospered during this time. In 1905, he built a comfortable house on Main Street, the popular choice for the well-to-do.

A two-story frame structure with cross-gables and numerous bays, its style is transitional, between Queen Anne and Neoclassical. Dominated by a broad, columned first-floor porch, its most arresting feature is the meticulously restored interior woodwork.

The house was placed on the National Register in 1987; in 1991, John and Valerie Tulip bought it, and built a large banquet and guest facility in the rear.

They are proud of the Statesboro Inn's eclectic food, honoring the seasons and several cultures. Popular at lunch are hot croissant sandwiches or specials such as homemade lasagne; dinner offers entrées of fresh fish—at least three choices—plus veal, chicken, a shrimp-scallop combination, and their famous filet of tenderloin, all individually prepared, with creative sauces.

A lot of Belgian chocolate goes into desserts here; there's Pudding Cake (solidified hot fudge topped with ice cream), Kentucky Pie (more chocolate, with coconut and pecans), and the signature Profiterole, a homemade cream puff filled with ice cream and drenched in melted Belgian chocolate. Ask for "Peterson's Delight" and they'll add fresh strawberries.

The Statesboro Inn and Restaurant, 106 S. Main Street, is about 13 miles off I-16; use exit 25 eastbound, exit 26 westbound. Statesboro is 50 miles northwest of Savannah, 76 miles southwest of Augusta. The restaurant is open for lunch 11:30 a.m. to 1:30 p.m., Tuesday through Friday; dinner, Tuesday through Saturday, is 6 to 9 p.m. (912)489-8628. Dress is "golf to tuxedo," wine and beer are available, and reservations are usually necessary. Busiest times are during events related to Georgia Southern University. There are 15 overnight units. AE,DC,DS,MC,V. ($$)

CRAB CAKES

1 pound crab claw meat	1 egg
¼ cup minced scallions	½ teaspoon dry mustard
¼ cup minced green pepper	1 teaspoon capers (optional)
About 1 cup bread crumbs	Salt and pepper
	Herb or seasoned butter

In bowl, mix all ingredients and form cakes about 2" across. Sauté to brown in butter. Place on shallow pan and bake at 400 degrees 7 to 10 minutes. Serve on pool of Tarragon Sauce.

TARRAGON CREAM SAUCE

½ teaspoon minced shallots	1 Tablespoon tarragon
2 Tablespoons wine vinegar	1½ cups heavy cream
2 Tablespoons white wine	½ teaspoon Dijon mustard

In saucepan, mix first 4 ingredients and reduce liquid. Add cream and mustard, bring to boil, then simmer until thickened. Yields about 1½ cups.

BANANA PANCAKES

1½ cups self-rising flour
2 Tablespoons sugar
⅛ teaspoon cinnamon
2 eggs, beaten

2 Tablespoons
  melted butter
About ¾ cup milk
⅓ cup mashed banana
Garlic butter*

In large bowl, mix dry ingredients; add liquids and mix well. Stir in banana; if too thick, add more milk. Coat griddle with garlic butter,* spoon out ¼ cup batter and cook until bubbles form; flip and finish. Yields 6-8 pancakes.

*Chef's note: this is NOT a typo.

BONNIE'S DELIGHT

12 ounces premium Belgian
  semi-sweet chocolate
1½ cups butter

⅜ cup heavy cream
7 eggs, separated
⅜ cup sugar, sifted with
  1 cup flour

In top of double boiler, melt first 3 ingredients together. In bowl of mixer, place yolks and slowly add flour mixture, then add chocolate mixture. In clean bowl, whip egg whites until stiff but not dry, then fold into chocolate mixture. Pour into springform pan and bake at 325 degrees 40 minutes; it should appear slightly undercooked. Serve warm and soft with vanilla ice cream, if desired.

Chef's note: this will freeze several months or refrigerate 1 week. Heat in microwave 20 to 30 seconds to serve.

THE OLDE PINK HOUSE
Savannah

J ames Edward Oglethorpe, appalled by English debtors' prisons, petitioned George II to charter a thirteenth colony in which bankrupt people could start a new life producing silks, wines, and spices for English consumption.

On February 12, 1733, one hundred twenty-five "poor people of good moral character," few actually debtors, landed at a high bluff on the Savannah River. The town they laid out, with wide shady streets and garden-like squares, was one of the first planned cities in North America, and remains one of the most beautiful.

Georgia's Sons of Liberty included three sons of early settler James Habersham: Joseph, John, and James. On Reynolds Square, James built a handsome two-story, Georgian-style house of brick covered with stucco; the house acquired its color when the brick bled through.

In 1812, the house became The Planters' Bank; it was altered and enlarged, and vaults were built in the basement. The Greek Revival portico was added about 1820.

Poverty following the War Between the States helped save Savannah. When preservation began in the 1950s, many buildings were restored, and Savannah's Historic District was named a National Historic Landmark in 1966.

The Habersham house was painstakingly restored in 1970. Underpinnings were strengthened to level sloping floors, an attic staircase duplicating the missing main stair was lowered into its place, vaults that once hid Confederate silver were opened, and fireplaces were uncovered.

Since 1971, the Olde Pink House Restaurant has served delectable "Low Country" and Southern Colonial foods in four period dining rooms and in the quaint basement tavern, where flickering candles and open fires remind you of Georgia's early days.

Feast on Ogeechee Mull, Veal Thomas Jefferson (with local crab and shrimp in Bearnaise), or Mr. and Mrs. Habersham's five-course dinner for two, featuring Chateaubriand or Rack of Lamb. For a modern taste, the day's catch might be baked salmon with apricot-lime glaze, served over spinach tortellini.

Despite a great assortment of desserts, few can resist the Pink House's famed Trifle, fragrant with sherry and rich with cream.

The Olde Pink House, 23 Abercorn Street, is open 7 days a week. Lunch is 11:30 a.m. to 2:30 p.m., Monday through Saturday, and dinner is 5:30 to 10 p.m. (912)232-4286. All legal beverages are available, dress is "nice casual" to more formal, and reservations are preferred. AE,MC,V. ($$$)

OGEECHEE MULL*

3 Tablespoons butter, divided
1 cup sliced mushrooms
½ cup chopped onion
½ cup chopped green pepper
¼ cup chopped celery
2 cups small shrimp, peeled, deveined, and cooked
2 cups diced cooked ham
2 cups diced cooked chicken or turkey
16-ounce can tomatoes, chopped
½ teaspoon salt
¼ teaspoon pepper
1 Tablespoon sugar
Dash Tabasco
1 Tablespoon flour
1 cup chicken stock
½ cup olive oil OR bacon drippings
Cooked rice
Chopped parsley and lemon slices

In stockpot, melt 2 Tablespoons butter, and sauté next 4 ingredients. Stir in next 8 ingredients and simmer 15 to 20 minutes, or until thickened, stirring occasionally. Mix flour with some liquid from pot; add with remaining butter, stock and oil OR drippings and simmer 20 minutes. Adjust seasonings; serve over rice, garnished with parsley and lemon. Serves 4 to 6.

PHYLLIS' FLUFFY YEAST ROLLS*

2 packages dry yeast
1 cup sugar
1 teaspoon salt
4 eggs, beaten
About 8½ cups flour, sifted
1 cup shortening, melted
2 Tablespoons melted butter

Dissolve yeast in 1 cup warm water. In large bowl, combine with sugar, salt, and 3 cups warm water. Add eggs and mix well; add flour and blend until dough is smooth, adding more flour if necessary. Knead in shortening. Place dough in large greased bowl, brush with melted butter, and turn to coat entire surface. Cover and store in refrigerator. When ready to make rolls, divide dough into small fat strips and circle into muffin pan. Cover and set in warm place to rise about 2 hours, or until doubled. Bake at 350 degrees 18 to 20 minutes, or until golden brown. Serve immediately. Yields about 3 dozen.

PINK HOUSE TRIFLE*

6 cups milk
1½ cups sugar
2 Tablespoons corn starch
6 eggs
½ cup sherry

1½ pounds pound cake, sliced
Raspberry or strawberry preserves
2 cups heavy cream, whipped

In top of double boiler, heat milk. In large bowl, beat together sugar, corn starch, and eggs until smooth. Add to milk and heat, stirring, until thickened. Cool. Add sherry to cooled custard. In serving bowl or individual glass dishes, arrange cake slices spread with preserves. Top with layer of custard, then layer of whipped cream. Repeat with all ingredients, ending with cream. Chill. Serves 6 to 8.

*From *Recipes From The Olde Pink House,* Copyright © 1981. Used by permission.

MRS. WILKES' BOARDING HOUSE
Savannah

General Oglethorpe's plan for Savannah has been called "one of the most outstanding works of architecture in American history." Laid out as four wards arranged around four central squares, the town grew to encompass twenty-four such squares, twenty-two of which remain.

The clapboard cottages of 1733 were followed by three-story Georgian and Federal houses with English basements, their front doors high above noisy, dusty streets, reached by graceful curving stairs. Reflecting the prosperity that came to Savannah after the war of 1812, these comfortable, elegant houses became the standard.

As Savannah grew toward the south, houses were frequently "paired," or built as rows, grouped around pleasant park-like squares or facing each other across dignified streets.

Some houses on Jones Street date from the early 1850s, and the street appears on an 1856 map, but the paired houses at 105-107 West Jones were built by Algernon S. Hartridge about 1870. Of Savannah grey brick, they are three stories over a ground-level basement, with double stairs and cast iron trim.

In 1965, they were the first houses sold in the Pulaski Square restoration project, purchased by Mr. and Mrs. L.H. Wilkes, who had run a boarding house there for years. The houses are included in the Savannah Historic District, named a National Historic Landmark in 1966.

Mr. and Mrs. Wilkes had left their home town of Vidalia in the 1940s, and moved to Savannah, where he worked for the Seaboard Railroad. They lived in the boarding house operated at that time by Mrs. Dennis Dixon; when she became ill, Mrs. Wilkes helped her, learned from her, and eventually bought the business.

Now occupying the entire basement, the restaurant is entered through a door on the right side. A tiny sign near the curb is a recent concession; Mrs. Wilkes never advertises, preferring people to feel they are guests in her home.

And what a hostess she is! Guests are ushered, in appropriate numbers, to large tables laden with the best of traditional Southern cooking. At breakfast, heaping platters of eggs, bacon, homemade sausage, ham, grits, and old-fashioned biscuits sate the sharpest appetite.

Luncheon fare might be fried chicken, pork chops, beef stew, candied yams, black-eyed peas, turnip greens, and tomato and okra gumbo, with corn bread muffins, plenty of iced tea, and a choice of delicious desserts, all prepared to perfection.

It is no wonder Mrs. Wilkes has been invited to serve her food all over the world, and is beloved by Savannahians and tourists alike.

A word of advice: go early and often.

Mrs. Wilkes' Boarding House, 107 W. Jones Street, is open Monday through Friday. Breakfast is 8 to 9 a.m., and lunch is 11 a.m. to 3 p.m.; it is closed the first two weeks in July. (912)232-5997. Dress is casual, reservations and credit cards are not accepted; personal checks accepted. ($)

TOMATO AND OKRA GUMBO*

2 pounds baby okra,　　½ teaspoon salt
　fresh or frozen　　　1 Tablespoon margarine
28-ounce can tomatoes　3 slices bacon, diced

Cut okra in ½" pieces. In saucepan, pour tomatoes, add okra and remaining ingredients. Cover and cook over medium heat 20 minutes. Serves 8.

SQUASH CASSEROLE*

4 pounds yellow squash, sliced　4 ounces margarine
1 medium onion, sliced　　　　1 cup undiluted canned
1 teaspoon pepper　　　　　　　mushroom soup
1 Tablespoon salt　　　　　　　1 cup grated American cheese
　　　　　　　　　　　　　　　　for topping

In saucepan, cook squash and onion in ½ cup water over medium heat about 20 minutes. Drain. Mash and add other ingredients, place in greased baking dish and top with cheese. Bake at 350 degrees 20 minutes.

SWEET POTATO SOUFFLÉ*

4 pounds sweet potatoes
1 teaspoon salt
1½ cups sugar
2 eggs
½ cup raisins
Grated rind and juice of
   1 lemon

½ teaspoon nutmeg
½ cup evaporated milk
½ cup chopped pecans
4 ounces butter
½ cup shredded coconut
Marshmallows

Slice potatoes and boil in salted water until tender. Mash and whip potatoes, add remaining ingredients, and pour into greased casserole. Bake at 350 degrees 30 minutes; cover top with marshmallows, brown, and serve.

FRIED CHICKEN*

2½ pound fryer, cut up
Salt and pepper

2 Tablespoons
   evaporated milk
Flour
Oil

Season chicken with salt and pepper; mix milk with 2 Tablespoons water and sprinkle over chicken. Allow to sit 20 minutes. Dredge chicken in flour, shake off excess, and deep fry at 300 degrees or pan fry over medium heat. Make sure chicken is covered with oil at all times. Fry until golden brown. Same recipe may be used for pork chops.

*From *Famous Recipes from Mrs. Wilkes' Boarding House in Historic Savannah.* Copyright © 1976, Mrs. L. H. Wilkes. Used by permission.

ELIZABETH ON 37th
Savannah

The American Revolution in Georgia was a messy guerrilla war. Strikes against opposing sides were made by quasi-military groups with personal grudges, factions within Continental forces squabbled among themselves, and ineptly defended Savannah fell to the British almost without resistance.

Eighty-two years later, Union General W.T. Sherman made his land-scorching "march to the sea" from Atlanta, destroying homes, crops, churches, and all food supplies and livestock.

Again, poorly defended Savannah, weak from a two-year blockade, capitulated. The city sustained relatively light damage; occupation by Union forces was peaceful, and recovery after Reconstruction was quick.

Savannah grew toward the south, following a grid pattern that echoed earlier development. About 1900, the Gibbes family, successful cotton brokers, built a home on 37th Street similar to one seen in Boston. With some elements of Beaux Arts and Italian Renaissance styles, the 2-story stucco house is an impressive corner landmark.

Elizabeth and Michael Terry, seeking a less hectic life than Atlanta offered, bought the house in 1980 and remodeled it to include living quarters upstairs and a restaurant on the first floor.

Your first clue to Elizabeth's attitude is the fragrant herb garden in the front yard. Food is foremost here, and you're in for a gastronomic adventure you will long remember.

Think about Vidalia onions stuffed with spicy Italian sausage and sharp cheddar in a lemon butter sauce; or roasted eggplant with shrimp; or sautéed flounder and cobia with roasted new potatoes and yellow squash casserole. Imagine lamb chops accompanied by a lamb patty centered with Georgia goat cheese; or oysters and mushrooms in piecrust with country ham and cream.

Not to be missed are the no-holds-barred desserts. Savannah cream cake is nutmeg-angelfood cake and sherry cream sauce, reformed and sliced, with puréed berry sauce. Pecan almond tart is served with bourbon caramel sauce and vanilla ice cream; and you can count on three chocolate desserts, each with a different texture, and all "such stuff as dreams are made on."

Elizabeth on 37th, 105 East 37th Street, is open Monday through Saturday for dinner from 6 p.m. In summer, the last reservation is 10 p.m., in winter, 9:30 p.m. (912)236-5547. All legal beverages are available, suggested dress is coat and tie for men, dresses for women, and reservations are STRONGLY recommended. The restaurant is closed 2 weeks at the end of summer. AE,MC,V. ($$$)

COUNTRY TOMATO AND RED PEPPER SOUP

1 sweet red pepper, skinned, seeded, and chopped
1-pound can diced tomatoes in juice OR 1½ pounds fresh tomatoes, peeled, seeded, and diced
4 Tablespoons extra virgin olive oil, divided
½ cup Vidalia or Spanish onion, diced
½ cup eggplant, peeled and diced
¼ cup pacilla pepper, seeded and diced
Large clove garlic, minced
4 cups chicken stock
1 cup minced zucchini
1 teaspoon minced garlic
2 Tablespoons fresh basil, minced
1 Tablespoon cider vinegar
Salt and pepper
1 pound small shrimp, peeled and deveined, optional

In large pot, place prepared red pepper and tomato. In sauté pan, in 2 Tablespoons oil, sauté onion until soft. Add next 3 ingredients and sauté until eggplant is soft; add to pot with stock and bring to boil, then simmer 15 minutes. Purée in batches in blender or food processor. In skillet, warm remaining oil, add zucchini and garlic and sauté to crisp-tender; DO NOT BROWN. Add to warmed soup with basil and vinegar. Season. Add optional shrimp for heartier soup. May be served hot or chilled. Serves 6.

SAVANNAH GINGERED CHEESE PUDDING

*Crust - prepare ahead
**Sauce - prepare ahead
9 ounces fresh ricotta cheese
⅓ cup sugar
5 Tablespoons lemon juice
½ cup sour cream

2 Tablespoons Grand
  Marnier or orange juice
1 Tablespoon gelatin
¼ cup warm water
2 cups heavy cream,
  whipped

In large bowl, whisk first 5 ingredients to blend. Set aside. In small cup, sprinkle gelatin over water and set into simmering waterbath; stir to dissolve. Whisk gelatin into cheese mixture; fold in cream. Spoon pudding into prepared molds* and refrigerate at least 3 hours. To serve, run knife around each mold; turn puddings out onto dessert plates. Sprinkle 1 Tablespoon reserved crumbs on top of each; ring puddings with sauce.** Serves 10.

*Crust: In food processor, combine 7 ounces broken Swedish gingersnaps, ⅓ cup sugar, 4 ounces melted butter, and 2 Tablespoons minced candied ginger. Process until crumbs resemble coarse meal. Sprinkle 1 Tablespoon crumbs into bottom of ten ½-cup molds. Reserve remaining crumbs.

**Sauce: In food processor, combine 10-ounce package frozen blackberries or raspberries, thawed, OR 1 pint fresh berries, with 2 Tablespoons sugar and 4 Tablespoons Grand Marnier or orange juice. Process and set aside.

BOBBIE'S DINER
SAVANNAH COLLEGE
OF ART AND DESIGN
Savannah

Savannah's enduring charm and grace, based on its original plan and individual style of architecture, might have been lost for all time, but for a few determined people.

In the early 1950s, the City Market was razed and replaced by a parking garage; in 1955, the 1820 Davenport House, on Columbia Square, was threatened with demolition. Its rescue became part of an effort to save the entire historic area, and a revolving fund was established to restore additional structures.

Today, the 2.2 square mile National Historic Landmark is one of the largest districts in the country, covering more than 2,000 buildings, most of them restored. Restoration of the Victorian District, which began in the 1970s, continues.

Preservation is not just about houses, or important edifices, or limited to the very old. Buildings of all types and ages have contributed to our cultural heritage; even Savannah, where preservation has been so successful, still has plenty of historic structures awaiting restoration.

THE STREAMLINER

Some of Savannah's more unwieldy buildings—a jail, schools, a bank, office buildings, and a Scottish Rite Temple—have been restored and adapted for unexpected use as studios, classrooms, and dormitories for the Savannah College of Art and Design.

Beginning in 1979 with 71 students and the restoration of the 1892 three-story Richardsonian Romanesque Savannah Volunteer Guards Armory, "SCAD" has renovated more than 30 derelict buildings, and has grown to an enrollment of twenty-five hundred.

Because classrooms are so scattered, SCAD provides transportation in double-decker London buses, and food service in a bookstore/café (a former drug store)—and two classic diners on vacant lots near classrooms.

The Streamliner was manufactured by the Worcester Lunch Car Company, Worcester, Massachusetts, in 1938. With original mauve marble counters, green stained-glass windows, and oak and birch woodwork, it seats thirty-six. There's even a period jukebox that plays period records.

Bobbie's Diner, built by Mountain View Diners, Mountain View, Rhode Island, in the 1950s, seats thirty-one in its blue-and-white tile and stainless steel interior, and has the appeal of the rock 'n roll era. Both diners have kitchen additions and accessible restrooms that meet modern code requirements, and are open to the public as well as to students.

You can still get breakfast all day (with grits and Mrs. Wilkes' fat biscuits); soda-fountain treats (and bottled mineral water); and blue-plate or Bobbie's Specials (meat, two vegetables, and bread); but hot dogs are all-beef; burgers and sandwiches come with your choice of white, wheat, or rye breads, Kaiser rolls or buns; and baked potatoes are as available as french fries.

Top quality meats, Graffeo coffee from San Francisco, milkshakes made with Ghiradelli chocolate, and homemade cakes and brownies make the diners up-to-date.

The "good old days" were never THIS good.

BOBBIE'S DINER, 1402 Habersham Street, is at the corner of Anderson; it is open Monday through Thursday 10 a.m. to 8 p.m., Friday 10 a.m. to 5 p.m., and Saturday 10 a.m. to 3 p.m. (912)238-2443. THE STREAMLINER, at the corner of Barnard and West Henry streets, is most easily reached from downtown by Abercorn Street, south to Henry Street; turn right, and The Streamliner will be on your right. It is open Monday through Saturday, 8 a.m. to 8 p.m. (912)238-2447. At both diners, dress is casual, and neither reservations nor credit cards are accepted. ($)

STREAMLINER POTATO SALAD

3 pounds potatoes, peeled, cooked, & diced
½ cup chopped celery
½ cup chopped green pepper

3 hard-cooked eggs, cubed
1 cup sour cream
2 teaspoons mayonnaise
1 teaspoon mustard
1 teaspoon catsup

In large bowl, blend all ingredients together. Refrigerate until ready to serve.

BOBBIE'S DINER FUDGE BROWNIES

½ cup butter or margarine
Two 1-ounce squares
  unsweetened chocolate
1 cup sugar

2 eggs
1 teaspoon vanilla
¾ cup sifted flour
½ cups chopped walnuts

In saucepan, melt butter and chocolate over low heat. Remove from heat; stir in sugar. Cool slightly; blend in eggs, one at the time, then vanilla. Stir in flour and nuts and mix well. Spread in greased 8" square pan and bake at 350 degrees 30 minutes. Do not overbake. Cool and cut into squares.

BOBBIE'S DINER SOUTHERN PECAN PIE

9-inch unbaked pie shell
3 eggs
⅔ cup sugar

Dash salt
1 cup dark corn syrup
⅓ cup melted butter
1 cup pecan halves

In large bowl, beat eggs thoroughly with next 4 ingredients. Stir in pecans; pour into pie shell. Bake at 350 degrees 50 minutes or until knife inserted 2" from edge comes out clean.

JEKYLL ISLAND CLUB HOTEL
Jekyll Island

Captain William Horton, under orders from General Oglethorpe, established an outpost on Jekyll Island in 1736. Spanish troops, retreating after the Battle of Bloody Marsh in 1742, burned Horton's house, but he rebuilt and lived on the island until 1748.

In 1886, Jekyll became a private winter resort for such industrialists as Vincent Astor, Marshall Field, J.P. Morgan, Joseph Pulitzer, and William Vanderbilt. Some members of the Jekyll Island Club built individual "cottages," but many stayed in the Club House.

With a dairy, garden, laundry, library, and church, the island provided all comforts; members and their guests enjoyed riding, cycling, tennis, hunting, picnicking and golf.

A tanker in nearby St. Simons Sound was torpedoed by a German submarine in 1942, and the island was evacuated. The era had ended, and the club never reopened.

The island was purchased by the state of Georgia in 1947, and the playground of millionaires became a popular state park. There are twenty miles of biking trails, 63 holes of golf, shelling, crabbing, shrimping, sailing and deep-sea fishing, with special planned recreation for children.

Many "cottages" have been restored, and the 240-acre Jekyll Island Club Historic District, placed on the National Register in 1972, was declared a National Historic Landmark in 1978.

The Club House, an enormous, fanciful Victorian structure replete with turrets, porches, and balconies, was renovated and enlarged in 1987 to become a luxury hotel. Beneath the Grand Dining Room's gleaming white columns, guests savor individually prepared dishes that reflect the history and flavor of the region.

At lunch, choose the preparation of your fresh catch; enjoy popular sautéed crab cakes on English muffins, oozing with melted cheese; or perhaps you'd prefer a salad with a special soup— Farmer's Pot is a hearty vegetable with smoked ham.

Dinner entrées include Veal Française and Lobster Américaine, reflecting Jekyll's golden years, while Pan-Blackened Medallions of Pork Loin with cinnamon-rum apple sauce and Shrimp San Remo (sautéed with sun-dried tomatoes, artichoke hearts, mushrooms and onions in rosemary sauce) appeal to more modern tastes.

Select your own entrée at Sunday Brunch, then browse among tables filled with delicacies—more than 20 different desserts—and you, too, will feel like a millionaire.

The Jekyll Island Club Hotel, a Radisson Resort, is open 7 days a week. In the Grand Dining Room, breakfast is 7 to 11 a.m., to 10 a.m. Sunday; lunch is 11:30 a.m. to 2 p.m., Monday through Saturday; Sunday brunch is 10:45 a.m. to 2 p.m.; dinner is 6 to 10 p.m. (912)635-2600. All legal beverages are available. Daytime dress is casual; coats and reservations are expected for dinner. Advance reservations advised for holidays and special occasions. There are 134 overnight units in 3 historic buildings. AE,CB,DC,DS,MC,V. Breakfast and lunch ($$), dinner ($$$).

ROAST GARDEN SALAD

8 ounces olive oil	8 mushrooms
4 ounces balsamic vinegar	½ sweet red pepper, roasted,
Dash Italian seasoning	skinned, in julienne
½ ounce chopped garlic	Romaine lettuce, washed
12 ounces zucchini, sliced	2 tomatoes, quartered
6 ounces yellow squash, sliced	4 ounces Asiago cheese, grated

In bowl, stir together oil, vinegar, and seasonings. Coat squash with oil mixture, lay on hot grill until dark marks appear, repeat on other side, chill. Dip mushrooms in oil mixture, sauté, and chill. To assemble, place lettuce on 4 plates; divide vegetables among plates, and top with grated cheese. Serves 4.

CHICKEN À LA MILANAISE

Six boneless, skinless
   chicken breasts
1½ cups seasoned flour
1 egg, beaten
1½ cups seasoned
   bread crumbs
Oil

4½ ounces diced tomato
3 ounces diced scallion
1½ ounces chopped garlic
3 dashes seasoning salt
Chopped parsley
6 ounces heavy cream
4½ ounces butter, cubed

Pound breasts, dredge in flour, dip in egg, then in bread crumbs. In skillet over high heat, sauté each breast on 1 side in oil. Turn breasts over in shallow pan and finish cooking in 500 degree oven. In same skillet, toss vegetables and garlic until tomatoes start to break down. Add seasoning salt and parsley and toss; stir in cream and butter and heat. Serve breasts topped with sauce. Serves 6.

PASTA ALFREDO

11 ounces cooked pasta
12 ounces heavy cream
½ ounce chopped garlic
Seasoning salt

Chopped parsley
3 ounces grated
   Asiago cheese
2 ounces butter
Grated Asiago cheese

In large hot sauté pan, place cream with garlic, salt, and parsley and heat to a boil. Add pasta, toss until pasta is hot, remove from heat and add cheese and butter. Serve with additional cheese. Serves 4.

SEAGLE'S IN THE RIVERVIEW
St. Marys

Colonial Georgia was divided into eight parishes in 1758; seven were named for saints, and the one including Savannah was called "Christ Church." After Creek Indian cessions in 1763, the colonial border moved south to the St. Marys River, and four new parishes were named in 1765.

Following the Revolution, parishes were made into counties. Camden County was created from St. Mary and St. Thomas, and the temporary seat was the town of St. Marys, which was laid out on Buttermilk Bluff, the site of an Indian village, in 1788.

The resulting town, with wide streets and gracious old buildings, has been an important port at different times in the state's history, including today, when a nuclear submarine base occupies nearby Kings Bay, and the ferry for the Cumberland Island National Seashore stops at the town dock.

The Riverside Hotel, built in 1916, is a two-story, flat-roofed structure with strong exterior walls of local sandstone brick, and a two-story veranda overlooking town and river. Operated as a hotel by the Brandon family from 1927 until 1959, it was closed until 1975, when the National Park Service opened Cumberland Island and a new generation of the family took over the hotel.

The building was given a protective coat of stucco in 1976, when the corner drugstore became the dining room. That same year, as part of the St. Marys Historic District, it was placed on the National Register.

Seagle's in the Riverview, a comfortable, relaxed restaurant with exposed-brick walls, large windows, and bustling waitresses, draws a clientele of local people and back-packers bound for Cumberland Island.

Entered through the heart-pine hotel lobby, it is the quintessential riverside seafood restaurant, serving products unloaded at the dock across the street, plus Louisiana crawfish. Local rock shrimp and Atlantic shrimp are the specialty. "We'll serve them any way anybody wants to eat them, including blackened," said current owner Jerry (Mayor of St. Marys) Brandon.

A combination platter including oysters, scallops, shrimp, rock shrimp, deviled crab, fish, potato, cole slaw, and hush puppies is typical of Seagle's generous servings at moderate prices, but you'll frequently find flounder, sea trout, grouper, and red snapper.

With a glass of superb iced tea, a piece of homemade pie, and a lazy day before you, what more can you ask?

193

Seagle's in the Riverview Hotel, 105 Osborne Street, is open 7 days a week. Breakfast is 7 to 11 a.m., lunch, Monday through Friday (possibly Saturday) is 11 a.m. to 2 p.m., and dinner is 5:30 to 10 p.m. Monday through Saturday, until 9 p.m. Sunday. (912)882-4187; Hotel (912)882-3242. St. Marys is 30 miles south of Brunswick and 30 miles north of Jacksonville, Florida. Dress is casual, all legal beverages are available (except Sunday) and reservations are accepted only for groups of 10 or more. There are 18 overnight units. AE,DC,DS,MC,V, Personal checks. ($)

FRIED SHRIMP

Large shrimp, peeled,
   deveined, and butterflied
AND/OR
Rock shrimp, peeled,
   with tails removed

1 egg, beaten with
   3 ounces milk
Flour
Peanut oil
Spicy cocktail sauce
   and lemon wedge

Dip shrimp in egg/milk mixture carefully; dredge lightly in flour, and fry in 350 degree oil about 90 seconds, or until tender. Serve with cocktail sauce and lemon wedge.

CHOCOLATE BOURBON PIE

9-inch unbaked pie shell
2 eggs
4 ounces butter, melted
1 teaspoon vanilla
1 cup chopped pecans
3 teaspoons
   bourbon whiskey

1 cup sugar
½ cup flour
¾ cup chocolate chips
Whipped cream and
   stemmed maraschino
   cherry

In large bowl, beat eggs; beat in remaining ingredients one at the time, in order. Pour into pie shell and bake at 350 degrees 40 to 60 minutes, or until firm. Serve warm, topped with whipped cream and maraschino cherry.

RUM PIE

9-inch graham cracker
   crust, baked and cooled
1 envelope
   unflavored gelatin
¼ cup dark rum

3 egg yolks
6 Tablespoons sugar
⅞ cup heavy cream,
   whipped with
   ½ teaspoon vanilla
Grated chocolate

In small bowl over hot water, dissolve gelatin in ½ cup water. Add rum and set aside. In large bowl, beat egg yolks until fluffy. Beat in sugar, then gelatin mixture. Cool in refrigerator, stirring occasionally, until almost set. Fold into whipped cream, and pour into shell. Garnish with chocolate, and chill until set.

THE IRON ROSE
Douglas

$\mathbf{A}$s population grew in Georgia's "Wiregrass" country, a new county was carved from Appling, Telfair, and Irwin Counties in 1854. Named for John Coffee, a General in the Creek Indian War, State Senator, and Congressman, it was settled primarily by farmers from Virginia and the Carolinas.

Douglas, the county seat, was laid out on a 50-acre tract, and named for Stephen A. Douglas, Illinois Democrat, whose defeat by Abraham Lincoln in 1860 would be one of the factors contributing to the War Between the States.

Initial growth in the county was slow, brought to a standstill by the War, and its generous stand of fine yellow pine, although cut and floated down the Ocmulgee and other streams by small operations, was not viewed as a viable resource until the railroads came through in the late 1860s.

For about 80 years, the county's economy was dependent upon large lumber mills, but poor harvesting and marketing practices eventually made timber cutting unprofitable for all but the smaller companies. In recent years, there has been renewed interest, and reforestation has produced a pleasant mix of agricultural products in the area.

By 1930, Douglas was a town of 5,000, with attractive neighborhoods surrounding a prosperous downtown. About four blocks west of the courthouse, a comfortable bungalow was home to a family of teachers.

Purchased by Laverne Faulkner Martin, it was remodeled to contain a beauty shop, health spa, and restaurant; Laverne and her brother, Dorman Faulkner, took over the restaurant operation in early 1992, and converted the large spa rooms to banquet facilities.

The rest of the charming little house has cozy rooms with five or six tables each, and is decorated in pastels and chintz fabrics, echoed in the exterior color of soft pink. The name comes from a wrought-iron decoration near the front door.

You'll feel right at home at the Iron Rose; it's the kind of house everyone has known well at one time or another, with a simple, homey atmosphere and friendly service—and good food!

Popular here at lunch are one-dish meals—seafood casserole, chicken-stuffed crêpes, sherry-sauced Shrimp Supreme over green noodles—all with fruit or vegetable salad and hot bread. At dinner, you'll find many of the same dishes, plus grilled salmon steak with

Béarnaise sauce, and Nebraska steaks. The house special Filet Mignon is specially aged and guaranteed fork-tender.

Among desserts are Chocolate Truffle Mousse, Almond Amaretto Mousse, Strawberries and Cream Cheesecake, and traditional English Trifle: sponge cake spread with raspberry jam, soaked in sherry custard, and slathered with whipped cream.

The Iron Rose, 501 W. Ward (GA 32 W.), is on the corner of Daughtry, and is open for lunch Monday through Friday, 11 a.m. to 2 p.m. Dinner is 6 to 10 p.m., Monday through Saturday, but dinner hours may vary. (912)384-2353. Dress is casual, all legal beverages are available, and reservations are accepted. MC,V. ($$)

BROCCOLI-RAISIN SALAD

1 bunch broccoli, washed
   and dried
4 ounces raisins

¼ cup bacon chips
   or crumbles
½ large onion, thinly sliced
Dressing (below)

Chop broccoli stems, divide florets, and place all in bowl. Add next 3 ingredients and toss well in dressing. Refrigerate; keeps well for several days.

Dressing: mix ½ cup mayonnaise with 2 or 3 Tablespoons red wine vinegar and 2 or 3 teaspoons sugar. Use just enough to moisten salad. Serves 4.

FRUITED CHICKEN SALAD

For each serving:

On plate, place shredded lettuce, top with generous amount of chopped cooked chicken, then grated Swiss cheese. Surround with seasonal fresh fruit, and sprinkle all with toasted sliced almonds. Serve with poppy seed dressing.

POPPY SEED DRESSING

¾ cup sugar
1 teaspoon dry mustard
½ teaspoon salt
⅓ cup white vinegar

1½ Tablespoons juice
   from grated onion
1 cup vegetable oil
1½ Tablespoons
   poppy seeds

In screw-top jar, combine first 4 ingredients. Add oil and shake; stir in poppy seeds and shake. Chill. Yields about one pint.

CHICKEN MORNAY ON BROCCOLI

1 bunch broccoli,
   divided into spears, and
   cooked crisp-tender
½ cup butter or margarine
½ cup flour
2 cups chicken stock
1 cup heavy cream
1 cup dry white wine

Salt and pepper
¼ teaspoon
   Worcestershire sauce
1 cup freshly grated
   Parmesan cheese
4 cups diced cooked chicken
Additional grated cheese
Chopped parsley

In skillet, melt butter, stir in flour, and cook until foamy. Add stock and cream, and cook, stirring, until thickened. Stir in wine, seasonings, and cheese. Divide broccoli and chicken into 6 dishes, pour sauce on top, and sprinkle with cheese. Bake at 350 degrees until bubbling. Sprinkle with chopped parsley. Serves 6.

GIULIO'S
Valdosta

Spanish priests, visiting their Indian missions, are credited with being the first regular European travelers through North Florida and South Georgia. A trail they used, expanded by settlers after the 1814 Indian Cession, became the stagecoach road to Macon.

Created in 1825, Lowndes County has had four seats: Franklinville, 1828, Lowndesville, 1833, Troupville, 1837, to be on the stage route, and Valdosta, 1860, when the railroad came through. Troupville was named for Governor Troup, and when the final change was made, the new town was named for his plantation, Val d'Osta.

Valdosta was eventually crossed by seven branch lines of three railroads, and the site of extensive railroad shops. Other industries—cotton, feed, and saw mills, peanut plants, and machine shops, were attracted, and the town was booming by the turn of the century.

A trolley system opened in 1898 made Valdosta the smallest city in the country to have public transportation. Many of the town's elaborate houses were built along the trolley tracks out Patterson Street.

About 1920, a large stucco bungalow was built on Patterson at the corner of Ann Street, for a Dr. Smith. A wide veranda and porte cochère echo the horizontal lines of the Prairie school, but the interior, with its graceful stair and high ceilings, has a Neoclassical feeling.

Its proximity to nearby hospitals made it a logical choice for doctors; at least two lived and practiced there. About 1950, probably during the ownership of a Dr. Saunders, the house was unfortunately moved to the rear of its lot to make room for a filling station, parts of the veranda were enclosed for additional office space, and its address was changed to Ann Street.

As part of the expanded North Patterson Street Historic District, the house was placed on the National Register in 1990. Rachael Giuly purchased it in 1987 and adapted it for restaurant use, utilizing a menu that includes Greek and Italian specialties, local favorites, steaks, and fresh seafoods.

At Giulio's, seafoods may be blackened, char-broiled, sautéed in olive oil, or baked, at your request. Two of the most popular are sautéed swordfish with herbs and lemon, and Greek-style baked red snapper with vegetables.

Frequent Specials include a combination plate of manicotti, lasagne, and meatballs; baked marinated pork tenderloin with Greek potatoes and vegetables; and big shells stuffed with ricotta and spinach.

Always available are enormous Greek salads, Spinach Pie, Moussaka (layered eggplant, beef, cheeses, and sauce), and Shrimp Santorini (large shrimp sautéed in wine and olive oil, with scallions, tomatoes, and feta cheese).

You can even choose an entire "Greek Supper" that includes appetizer, salad, soup, entrée, bread, and beverage at a special price.

Among desserts are amaretto and white chocolate/raspberry swirl cheesecakes, homemade cream pies, and Baklava—a traditional Greek pastry made of thin layers of crisp pastry and nuts, drenched in sweetness.

Giulio's, 105 E. Ann Street, is on the corner of Patterson, and is open Tuesday through Saturday, 5 to 10 p.m. (912)333-0929. Dress is "jeans to tuxedo," beer and wine are available, and reservations are accepted, preferred for parties of 8 or more. AE,MC,V. ($$)

STUFFED GRAPE LEAVES

Bottled grape leaves in brine	3 Tablespoons
3 pounds ground beef	chopped parsley
2 large onions, finely chopped	Salt and pepper
1½ cups raw rice	Olive oil
	Beef, lamb, or chicken stock

Drain leaves and rinse in cold water. In bowl, mix beef with next 3 ingredients; season to taste. To shape rolls, place a leaf smooth side down; put 1 teaspoon filling in center and roll up cigar-fashion, turning in edges to seal. Repeat. Place rolls in oiled baking pan, seam-side down and touching each other. Cover with stock, and bake at 350 degrees 1 hour. Serve hot or cold. Makes about 50 appetizers.

LENTIL SOUP

2 cups lentils
2 garlic cloves, peeled
   and crushed
1 large onion, diced
½ cup chopped celery

2 ripe tomatoes, crushed
¼ cup olive oil
2 cups chicken stock
6 cups water
Salt and pepper

In stockpot, place all ingredients; cover pot and bring to boil. Reduce heat and simmer 1 hour or until lentils are soft. Correct seasonings and serve. Serves 8 to 10.

TZATZIKI
(yogurt and cucumber sauce)

1 cucumber, peeled
1 garlic clove, crushed
1 cup plain yogurt

2 teaspoons lemon juice
1 teaspoon chopped dill
   or mint
Salt

Grate cucumber, and squeeze out excess water. In bowl, mix all ingredients, salting to taste. Serve as an accompaniment to fish, stuffed grape leaves, or vegetables. Yields about 1½ cups.

INDEX TO RECIPES

Kahlúa Cheesecake, The Public House on Roswell Square, 71
Key Lime Pie, Glen-Ella Springs Inn, 19
Lace Cookies, In Clover, 134
Lemon Chess Pie, Burns-Sutton House, 27
Lemon Ice Box Pie, The Victorian Tea Room, 143
Peach Cobbler, Billie's Blue Willow Inn, 103
Peach Pan Pie, The New Perry Hotel, 155
Pecan Delight, The Adairsville Inn, 55
Pink House Trifle, The Olde Pink House, 175
Pumpkin Cheesecake, Rudolph's on Green Street, 39
Rum Cake, Beall's 1860, 151
Rum Pie, Seagle's in the Riverview, 195
Southern Pecan Pie, Bobbie's Diner, 187
White Chocolate Mousse with Fresh Raspberry Sauce, J. Henry's, 131

EGG AND CHEESE DISHES
Cheese Soufflé, The New Perry Hotel, 154
Broccoli Quiche, Burns-Sutton House, 27
Macaroni and Cheese, Billie's Blue Willow Inn, 103
Sausage, Egg, and Cheese Casserole, Magnolia Tea Room, 91
Spinach and Feta Cheese in Phyllo Pastry, Trumps at the Georgian, 42

FRUITS
Apple Crisp, White Elephant Café, 119
Apple Praline Pie, Stovall House, 15
Curried Fruit, The New Perry Hotel, 155
Fresh Berries and Cheesecake in Phyllo, The Mansion, 86
Heavenly Hash, Twelve Savannah, 126
Peach Cobbler, Billie's Blue Willow Inn, 103
Peach Pan Pie, The New Perry Hotel, 155
Pineapple Relish, J. Henry's, 130

PASTA
Capelle D'Angelo, Tiberio, 59
Fettuccine a la Ashley, The Southern Trace, 34
Pasta Alfredo, Jekyll Island Club Hotel, 191
Pasta Angelica, White Elephant Café, 118
Petite Palace Pasta, Black Swan Inn, 158

PORK, VEAL, and LAMB
Pork and Chinese Vegetable Phyllo, Stovall House, 14
Rack of Lamb, Mongolian Style, La Maison on Telfair, 110
Veal Cabriolet, Lickskillet Farm, 62

Veal Maison, The 1839 Goetchius House, 146
Veal Scaloppine, Black Swan Inn, 159

POULTRY
Breast of Chicken with Morels and Blackberry Sauce, Windsor Hotel, 162
Breast of Duckling with Strawberries and Peppercorns, Windsor Hotel, 163
Caribbean Chicken Salad, Yesterday Café, 106
Chicken Ala Milanaise, Jekyll Island Club Hotel, 191
Chicken Dijon, Simmons-Bond Inn, 31
Chicken Mornay on Broccoli, The Iron Rose, 199
Fried Chicken, Mrs. Wilkes' Boarding House, 179
Fruited Chicken Salad, The Iron Rose, 198
Grilled Island Chicken, J. Henry's, 130
Herb-Grilled Chicken, Glen-Ella Springs Inn, 18
Honey-Lime Chicken with Peanuts, The Southern Trace, 35
Italian Chicken, Maple Street Mansion, 122
Kat's Chicken Salad, Finnigan's Junction, 99
Lemon Chicken, The Adairsville Inn, 54
Marinated Chicken Livers, The Public House on Roswell Square, 70
Roast Duckling with Pecan Stuffing, The 1839 Goetchius House, 147
Turkey Divan, Beall's 1860, 150

SALADS AND DRESSINGS
Broccoli-Raisin Salad, The Iron Rose, 198
Calamari Salad, Villa D'Este, 67
Fruited Chicken Salad, The Iron Rose, 198
Heavenly Hash, Twelve Savannah, 126
Kat's Chicken Salad, Finnigan's Junction, 99
Poppy Seed Dressing, The Iron Rose, 199
Roast Garden Salad, Jekyll Island Club Hotel, 190
Salad Dressing, The Public House on Roswell Square, 70
Shrimp Galucki, The Freight Room, 95
Slaw, Another Thyme, 50
Streamliner Potato Salad, The Streamliner, 186

SANDWICHES
Black Russian Sandwich, Simmons-Bond Inn, 31
Pacific Coast Line Sandwich, The Freight Room, 95

SAUCES
Blackening Spice, Radium Springs Lodge Restaurant, 166
Crème Anglaise, The Mansion, 87
Cucumber and Yogurt Sauce (Tzatziki), Giulio's, 203

Curry Sauce for Poached Salmon, Radium Springs Lodge Restaurant, 167
Mango Chutney Pecan Sauce, Radium Springs Lodge Restaurant, 167
Pesto Sauce, Tiberio, 59
Raisin Sauce for Baked Ham, Bulloch House, 139
Red Pepper Coulis, The Abbey, 83
Red Pepper Jelly, Radium Springs Lodge Restaurant, 166
Smoked Garlic Cream, The Abbey, 83
Tarragon Cream Sauce, Statesboro Inn, 170
Tzatziki (yogurt and cucumber sauce), Giulio's, 203
Walnut-Spinach Pesto, White Elephant Café, 118

SEAFOODS AND FRESH WATER FISH
Calamari Salad, Villa D'Este, 67
Chicago-style Shrimp de Jonghe, Simmons-Bond Inn, 30
Crab Cakes, Statesboro Inn, 170
Crab Cakes, Taylor's Trolley, 22
Crawfish Étouffée, Harry Bissett's, 47
Crêpes San Luis, Trumps at the Georgian, 42
Escargot with Smoked Garlic Cream, The Abbey, 82
Fried Shrimp, Seagle's in the Riverview, 194
Grilled Shrimp on Yellow Pepper Beurre, 1848 House, 74
Grouper Elizabeth, Old Vinings Inn, 79
Lobster Harrington, Taylor's Trolley, 23
Oyster Stew, Old Vinings Inn, 78
Oysters Imperial, La Maison on Telfair, 110
Salmon Mousse, In Clover, 134
Sautéed Frog Legs, Lickskillet Farm, 63
Scallops en Papillote, Rudolph's on Main Street, 38
Shrimp Galucki, The Freight Room, 95
Skillet-Blackened Scallops, Finnigan's Junction, 99
Smoked Salmon Cheesecake, 1848 House, 75
Smoked Salmon Tartare, The Partridge Inn, 114
Trout Amandine, Maple Street Mansion, 123
Trout Pecan, Glen-Ella Springs Inn, 18
Tuna in Black Bean Salsa, Old Vinings Inn, 79

SOUPS
Autumn Pumpkin Bisque, The Windsor Hotel, 162
Bacon, Lettuce, and Tomato Soup, Rudolph's on Green Street, 38
Butternut Squash Soup with Apple Purée, Tiberio, 58
Chicken and Rice Soup, The Victorian Tea Room, 142
Corn Chowder, Taylor's Trolley, 22
Country Tomato and Red Pepper Soup, Elizabeth on 37th, 182

Lentil Soup, Giulio's, 203
Ogeechee Mull, The Olde Pink House, 174
Oyster Stew, Old Vinings Inn, 78
Peanut Soup, Beal's 1860, 150
Potato and Tasso Soup, Harry Bissett's, 46
Tomato Basil Bisque, Magnolia Tea Room, 90
Turkey and Rice Soup, The Freight Room, 94

VEGETABLES
Braised Red Cabbage, Yesterday Café, 107
Candied Yams, Bulloch House, 139
Collard Greens, Billie's Blue Willow Inn, 102
Fried Chili Peppers, Finnigan's Junction, 98
Mango and Tomato Salad with Basil Curry Dressing,
   The Partridge Inn, 114
Maque Choux, Harry Bissett's, 46
Skillet Squash, Billie's Blue Willow Inn, 102
Squash Casserole, Mrs. Wilkes' Boarding House, 178
Squash Casserole, The Victorian Tea Room, 142
Streamliner Potato Salad, The Streamliner, 186
Stuffed Potatoes, Twelve Savannah, 126
Sweet Potato Casserole, The New Perry Hotel, 154
Sweet Potato Soufflé, Mrs. Wilkes' Boarding House, 179
Sweet Potato Soufflé, Twelve Savannah, 127
Tomato and Okra Gumbo, Mrs. Wilkes' Boarding House, 178
Vegetable Casserole, Stovall House, 14